Cambridge Elements ☰

Elements in England in the Early Medieval World
edited by
Megan Cavell
University of Birmingham
Rory Naismith
University of Cambridge
Winfried Rudolf
University of Göttingen
Emily V. Thornbury
Yale University

WRITING THE WORLD IN EARLY MEDIEVAL ENGLAND

Nicole Guenther Discenza
University of South Florida

Heide Estes
Monmouth University

CAMBRIDGE
UNIVERSITY PRESS

Shaftesbury Road, Cambridge CB2 8EA, United Kingdom

One Liberty Plaza, 20th Floor, New York, NY 10006, USA

477 Williamstown Road, Port Melbourne, VIC 3207, Australia

314–321, 3rd Floor, Plot 3, Splendor Forum, Jasola District Centre, New Delhi – 110025, India

103 Penang Road, #05–06/07, Visioncrest Commercial, Singapore 238467

Cambridge University Press is part of Cambridge University Press & Assessment, a department of the University of Cambridge.

We share the University's mission to contribute to society through the pursuit of education, learning and research at the highest international levels of excellence.

www.cambridge.org
Information on this title: www.cambridge.org/9781108932059

DOI: 10.1017/9781108943147

First published 2023

A catalogue record for this publication is available from the British Library

ISBN 978-1-009-45435-3 Hardback
ISBN 978-1-108-93205-9 Paperback
ISSN 2632-203X (online)
ISSN 2632-2021 (print)

Cambridge University Press & Assessment has no responsibility for the persistence or accuracy of URLs for external or third-party internet websites referred to in this publication and does not guarantee that any content on such websites is, or will remain, accurate or appropriate.

Writing the World in Early Medieval England

Elements in England in the Early Medieval World

DOI: 10.1017/9781108943147
First published online: August 2023

Nicole Guenther Discenza
University of South Florida

Heide Estes
Monmouth University

Author for correspondence: Nicole Guenther Discenza, ndiscenza@usf.edu

Abstract: The early medieval English were far more diverse and better connected to a broader world than often thought. Their writings reveal substantial interest in Europe, Asia, and Africa while they situated themselves firmly within Christian Europe. They drew many ideas from textual sources and filled out their conceptions from their own travels and interactions with visitors. Chronicles, histories, poetry, homilies, saints' lives, and occasionally maps tell of peoples and lands from the British Isles to their near neighbors in Scandinavia to such distant places as Jerusalem, North Africa, and India. They also imagined geographies that veered into the fantastic and vividly depicted hell, purgatory, and heaven. This Element provides insights about early medieval English who were engaged deeply in a variety of modes with other parts of their world. Both the connections and the divisions they constructed still have an impact today.

This Element also has a video abstract: Cambridge.org/Discenza/ Estes_abstract

Keywords: early medieval England, Anglo-Saxon England, geography, Old English, Anglo-Latin

ISBNs: 9781009454353 (HB), 9781108932059 (PB), 9781108943147 (OC)
ISSNs: 2632-203X (online), 2632-2021 (print)

Contents

Introduction

How did the world look to English people of the early Middle Ages, from about 500 to 1100? The answer, of course, would vary from one individual to the next. Yet even 1,000 years later, we can discern key commonalities in the mental pictures of the world that early English writers described. First, they found it fascinating. They wrote about the world right around them and about more distant peoples and places. They described the Earth as spherical, with three continents: Europe, Asia, and Africa. They knew best the lands closest to them, where they had connections through family, religion, and trade. Their sense of place became less detailed and precise as distance grew, and they did not always distinguish real places from imaginary lands.

Early medieval English people concentrated on peoples rather than places. They named kingdoms and cities, but they often preferred terms that referred to people: *Angelcyn* (English people) to *Englalond* (England), *Francena ric* (kingdom of the Franks) to *Francland* (Francia), *Indisc men* (Indian men) to *Indie* or *India* (India). They also generally focused more on inhabitants of a place, including animals, monsters, and hybrids, than on natural and built landscapes.

Their interest in peoples led them to construct race and ethnicity. They did not categorize peoples precisely as we do now, but their race-making has influenced later thinking to the present day. While English writers sometimes depicted European neighbors as having different customs, even strange ones, they rarely portrayed them as physically different. But they described Jews and some inhabitants of Asia and Africa as culturally and sometimes physically different from other Europeans.[1]

Finally, they preferred to depict the world in words rather than maps. Surviving sources for early medieval English ideas about the rest of the known world include few maps but many documentary and literary sources, including travel accounts. Charters and annals describe very local landscapes. Knowledge of the wider world often came from classical and biblical sources. The historian Bede (fl. ca. 700–35) takes care to document the sources of his information about places from his own monastery to Rome to the outskirts of heaven. Other writers are less concerned to cite authority and to distinguish among fact, fiction, and fantasy. The Beowulf manuscript depicts monsters and dragons close to home (and connected with the Hygelac of actual Scandinavian history) in *Beowulf*, and more distant creatures in the *Wonders of the East* and the *Letter of Alexander to Aristotle*, fantastic accounts of strange and monstrous humans and animals to be found beyond the boundaries of the known world.

---

[1] A forthcoming Element in the Cambridge Elements in England in the Early Medieval World series will deal more directly with race.

Early English views of the world matter partly because they continue to affect contemporary anglophone conceptions of space, place, race, ethnicity, and religious identity. Early ideas that were not carried forward to the present still matter because they are important to understanding the past and its texts, and to denaturalize how we see the world now. Crucially, early medieval English texts and occasionally maps can show us alternative ways to view the world, and with both contemporary and past perspectives in mind, we can find new ways of looking as well.

Early maps that survive offer a useful introduction to early medieval English understandings of the world. So-called T-O maps (for example, MS Royal 6 C I, folio 108 v, 1075–1100; see Figure 1) represent the Mediterranean Sea and the Nile and Don Rivers as a "T" inside an "O" outlining the continents with the east at the top, as was common in the Middle Ages.[2] Asia is at the top, Europe at bottom left, and Africa at bottom right. Outside the first "O," a second delineates the oceans and, according to contemporary geometry, indicates a sphere. Much more detailed than typical T-O maps, the Cotton World Map (MS Cotton Tiberius B.v, folio 56, 1025–50; see Figure 2) depicts oceans, rivers, mountains, and cities and names peoples, animals, and monsters alongside geographical features. In the original, surrounding oceans and the Mediterranean Sea are in gray, with other bodies of water in red; mountains are green.

The British Isles are near the bottom left corner of the Cotton World Map; only the mythical Thyle lies beyond them.[3] Brittannia wraps around Ireland (*Hibernia*) to the east and south. The map names Scotland (*Camri*), Kent (*Cantia*), and the cities of London (*Lundonia*) and Winchester (*Wintonia*). The Orkneys are north of Brittania and the Jutland Peninsula is just to the east. Across the Channel are South Britons (*Suðbryttas*). France or the Franks have no label, and the Iberian Peninsula seems to extend north of France almost to Britain; it is home to the Brigantia, a Celtic people. Like the map of England, the map of Italy contains much detail; cities include Verona, Rome, Pavia, and Ravenna. The map also names Finns (*Scridefinnas*), Slavs (*Sleswic* and *Sclavi*), and Huns (*Hunorum gens*).

Jerusalem is near the center of the Cotton World Map, with Bethlehem nearby; several biblical cities and tribes are named. To the east, the map identifies Babylonia, Mesopotamia, Asia Minor, and India ("in which there

---

[2] The British Library's open-access image of the Royal of the T-O map is at www.bl.uk/manu scripts/Viewer.aspx?ref=royal_ms_6_c_i_f108v and the Cotton World Map is at www.bl.uk /manuscripts/Viewer.aspxref=cotton_ms_tiberius_b_v!1_f056v. See also Foys, Crossley, and Wacha, 2020.

[3] The name Thyle would later become associated with Iceland, but to classical and early medieval authors before the Norman Conquest, it signified the ends of the Earth; see Kedwards, 2020, 127–41.

Figure 1 T-O Map (MS Royal 6 C I, folio 108v)
Source: © British Library Board,MS Royal 6 C I, folio 108v

are 44 peoples [*gens*]").[4] Asia includes mountains, rivers, and the Arabian Desert. A gap in the Red Sea is labeled "transitus Hebreorum" (the crossing of the Hebrews). A drawing of a lion (*hic sunt leones*, here are lions) is near the top left, the only drawing of an animal on the map. Asia is also home to "griphorum gens" (gryphon people, elsewhere identified as animals), as well as Gog and Magog, biblical individuals, tribes, or regions, identified in the Middle Ages with giants. The map extends as far east as Tabrobana (Taprabane in the Old English *Orosius*, later in this section), known today as Sri Lanka.

Africa includes Carthage, Tingis (modern Tangier), Alexandria, and Mauritania. Libya and Ethiopia are both identified with three different places. Africa is labeled "powerful, but also more abundant with beasts and full of serpents." South of the Nile are "barbarian" Gaetuli, "the peoples of Gaulolum, extending all the way to the ocean," and "cinocephales" (dog-headed ones): Africa includes people who are not fully human. The Cotton World Map does not offer accurate proportions or even relative directions in many places; England and Europe are both disproportionately large and Africa comparatively

---

[4] Latham, Howlett, and Ashdowne, 1975–2013, offer "race, nation" as the first definition for *gens*; it may not correspond exactly to modern Western notions of race, but the sense of distinction among peoples comes through. Nicole Lopez-Jantzen, 2019, distinguishes "race," a hierarchical system based on origins, from "ethnicity," classification without hierarchy.

Figure 2 Cotton World Map (MS Cotton Tiberius B.v, folio 56)
Source: DEA PICTURE LIBRARY/De Agostini via Getty Images

tiny.[5] Yet it sketches the outlines of the known world and gives a sense of Britain's place: large enough to be significant but near the edge of the known world. Though it is difficult to know how early medieval English writers understood the locations of Africa and Asia, they richly imagined their animal, monster, and human inhabitants, in texts that defined places outside of Europe in problematic ways that resonate into the present. Histories, homilies, saints' lives, and poetry developed these ideas in greater detail.

---

[5] The commonly used Mercator projection map today makes Western Europe look larger, and Africa smaller, than they really are.

A scrap of Latin lore found in two manuscripts characterizes the various peoples of the world with a single word each. As written in British Library manuscript Harley 3271, the passage reads:

> Victory belongs to the Egyptians, ill-will to the Jews, wisdom to the Greeks, barbarity (or savagery) to the Picts, cunning and strength to the Romans, liberality to the Langobards, appetite to the Gauls, arrogance and ferocity to the Franks, ire to the Britons, stupidity to the Saxons and Angles, and lust to the Irish. (Estes, 2012, 641)

This passage, a similar version of which survives in British Library manuscript Cotton Caligula A. xv, shows the early medieval English compartmentalizing peoples by supposed dispositions, anticipating racial and ethnic stereotyping that persists to this day. Intriguingly, English writers themselves described Saxons and Angles as "stupid" (or at least copied the description), suggesting disdain for their compatriots based on stereotypes.

Most sources address geography and peoples with more nuance. In the sections that follow, we analyze texts from several different genres with different purposes and expectations. Histories often advanced overarching narratives and, along with chronicles, claimed authority to represent the past accurately. Paulus Orosius, an Iberian priest, wrote *Historiarum adversum paganos libri vii* (*Seven Books of History against the Pagans*) in Latin shortly before 420 to argue that Christianity brought peace, not devastation, to Rome. It influenced Bede, Alfred, and anonymous English homilists and was adapted into Old English around 900 with abridgements and other changes (Bately, 1980). The translator retained much of the opening detailed geography of the known world, but made some updates and other changes, some accurate, some erroneous. The Northumbrian monk Bede in 731 completed his Latin *Historia ecclesiastica gentis anglorum* (*Ecclesiastical History of the English People*), centered on the conversion of peoples in England to Roman Christianity.[6] This text, invaluable for our knowledge of early medieval England, shows the perspective of a learned writer informed by classical, patristic, and earlier Insular writers who himself influenced later writers; more than 160 medieval manuscripts of the text still exist, and an Old English version was written around 900. Bede opens with a short geography of the British Isles. A set of texts called the *Anglo-Saxon Chronicle* was probably initially produced at the West Saxon court to give an account culminating with Alfred the Great, King of Wessex.[7] As copies

---

[6] We follow a common translation of the title here, but note that Harris, 2003, demonstrates that Bede frequently uses Angli for "Anglians" rather than the English as a whole.

[7] We avoid the term "Anglo-Saxon" (see later in this section) and so after this call the text the *Old English Chronicle* or simply the *Chronicle*.

were continued in different places, later entries sometimes diverged according to the interests of different communities or scribes.

Poetic and prose saints' lives and biblical adaptations often took considerable license with their sources in service to religious or literary agendas.[8] The vast majority of early English poems survive in just four manuscripts. The Junius manuscript (Krapp, 1931) comprises poetic adaptations of parts of Genesis, Exodus, and Daniel, followed by *Christ and Satan*, which narrates Satan's temptation of Jesus and Jesus' victory over Satan in hell. The Exeter Book (Krapp and Dobbie, 1936) contains both secular and religious poems, many quite short. The Vercelli Book (Krapp, 1932) contains poems, including *Elene* and *Andreas*, alongside prose homilies. Finally, the Beowulf manuscript includes the poems *Beowulf* and *Judith* (Dobbie, 1953), and the prose *Letter of Alexander to Aristotle*, *Wonders of the East*, and *The Passion of Saint Christopher* (Fulk, 2010). Dates of composition for Old English poems are disputed, but these four poetic codices were all written down in about a fifty-year period around the end of the tenth century. Biblical poems draw upon the Bible for authority, but the poets select portions, add and omit details, and give their own emphases, making different kinds of truth claims than the histories.

The Bible known to the English was a Latin translation of a third-century Christian redaction of the Hebrew scriptures, appropriated as the "Old Testament," in combination with gospels, letters, and other materials called the "New Testament." The Hebrew Scriptures, written by Jews living in Israel, codified the Israelites' laws alongside histories of kings and prophets. Some Jews living in the last century before the Common Era believed that certain passages presaged a savior and that Jesus (Hebrew "Joshua") filled that role.[9] But to the extent that Jews believe that the Bible predicts a redeemer, they envision a human political leader still to come. Christians believed that their interpretation of what they called the Old and New Testaments constituted the only truth. As Christianity grew in power, adopted by Constantine and subsequent Roman emperors, the presence of Jews who disputed the basic premise of their religion became increasingly problematic for Christians.

Jews may have been in early medieval England as individual slaves or traders; communities are attested in archaeological and documentary sources only after the Norman Conquest. The strong presence of Jews in Old English poetry and prose "is solely a textual phenomenon, a matter of stereotypes embedded in long-standing Christian cultural traditions" (Scheil, 2004, 7).

---

[8] For biblical books, we use roman type, and for the poems based on them, we use italic.

[9] We use "Common Era" (CE) and "Before the Common Era" (BCE) rather than language drawn from Christianity – that is, "Before Christ" (BC) and "Anno Domini" (AD, "the year of our Lord").

English travelers to Aachen, Rome, and Jerusalem likely encountered Jews as well as Muslims. Christian writing about Muslims in the early medieval period expressed antipathy based on religious difference, but often with less antagonism than that expressed toward Jews, and chiefly in documentary texts. The many homilies and poems describing Jewish perfidy in terms stronger even than the language of the Gospels may owe something to the religious situation of early medieval England. Though Christianity had become the religion of England's kings, there were backsliders, and the survival of place-names with pagan elements in areas more remote from towns suggests the persistence of pagan beliefs and practices quite a bit later than written records from the period would admit (Estes, 2007). Insistence on the alterity of the Jews allows the English to express a sense of identity: if their ancestors had been pagans, as remembered in *Beowulf*, and if some among them still held to older customs, at least they could be unified as *not* Jews.

What the English called themselves is complicated. Scholars studying the early Middle Ages in England have long called the period and its people "Anglo-Saxon." The term, along with "Anglo-Saxonists" for the people who study it, has been rightly critiqued, and scholars substituted "Old English" for "Anglo-Saxon" as the name of the language decades ago. "Anglo-Saxon" was little used by people of the period. Some mainland European writers used Latin forms of the term, leaving a score of surviving appearances from the fourth through sixteenth centuries, but almost none of them were English; Alcuin, who hailed from York but spent much of his adult life among the Franks, was exceptional in using the term.[10] It appears in just over three dozen Latin texts from early medieval England, virtually all charters, to refer to the king of the united kingdom of Anglians and West Saxons – not to all of what is now England. It occurs only three times in Old English, and two of those are in texts that also contain Latin. No form of "Anglo-Saxon" was ever in wide use by the English people during the early Middle Ages. The term became widespread only much later, among people looking back at the period.

Many of the name's original enthusiasts were men such as Thomas Jefferson, whose love for the people and language he called Anglo-Saxon was bound to his conception of them as uniquely suited for rational self-rule, from which he excluded Native Americans and Black people (Vernon, 2018, 3–5). That tradition neither began nor ended with Jefferson, and the terms "Anglo-Saxon" and "Anglo-Saxonist" have been and continue to be used by white supremacists as self-designations (Rambaran-Olm, 2018 and 2019; Wilton, 2020). Therefore, we do not use this term; instead, we call the people the early medieval English,

---

[10] Wilton, 2020, identified the occurrences in this paragraph.

the language Old English, and the aforementioned *Chronicle* the Old English *Chronicle*.

The *Dictionary of Old English* cites about 225 occurrences of "English" as an adjective and 350 as a noun. *Englisc* (with many spelling variations) referred to the language, to people living in England who claimed kinship with Germanic-speaking tribes, and to such people with Germanic kin who had moved elsewhere. Bede tells us in his *Ecclesiastical History* that "Anglorum siue Saxonum gens" (the race of the Angles or Saxons, Colgrave and Mynors, 1969) came from three powerful Germanic tribes: the Angles, Saxons, and Jutes (I.15). Bede's Latin *Angli* usually refers to Anglians, the descendants of the mainland Angles (Harris, 2003, 45–82); the Old English *Bede* translates this as *Ongol* or *Ongolþeod* (Rowley, 2011, 57–70).[11] Early English people also identified as Saxon, often combined with a direction such as *Eastseaxe* (East Saxon) or *Suþseaxe* (South Saxon).[12] Another name for the English is *Angelcyn*, which Sarah Foot argues King Alfred the Great (ruled 871–99) promoted in translations associated with his court to unite his original West Saxon subjects with Kentish people and Mercians who came under his rule; more than half of its more than 200 occurrences in the surviving Old English corpus appear in the *Chronicle* and more than a quarter in the Old English *Bede*. Foot comments that rhetoric did not mean full unity: "Those who might at times have defined themselves as English would simultaneously recognise other loyalties: to their king, to their lord, to a village, to a region" (1996). Crucially, the "English" were never a single race or ethnicity. The "Angli" who gave the people their name had migrated from mainland Europe and joined numerous other linguistic and ethnic groups and individuals from across Europe as well as Africa and the Middle East (Karkov, 2020, chapter 4).

This Element begins with England and moves outward, from the places most familiar to the English to those least known. Section 1 treats England and Scandinavia, whose inhabitants spoke languages similar to English, and some of whom raided England starting in the late eighth century and then settled there. England had close but fraught ties with Scandinavian neighbors and immigrants. Section 2 explores England's views of the rest of mainland Europe. Many English nobles and churchmen and -women had close ties to Franks in what are now France, Germany, and the Low Countries. Rome was a religious and political center in Europe. The English had contact with Eastern Europe and with Spain; some writers show hostility to Muslims living there.

---

[11] Old English spelling was not as fixed as Modern English, so "Angle" appears variously as *angel-*, *angl-*, *ongel-*, *ongl-*, and occasionally in other forms.

[12] Surviving today in the place-names Essex and Sussex.

Section 3 moves beyond Europe. Like Rome, Jerusalem was a religious center; unlike Rome, it had significant Jewish and Muslim populations. English writers were intrigued by what they considered holy lands around Jerusalem. They admired some men and women of the Hebrew Bible whom they considered exemplary, while presenting most Jews after the coming of Christianity as wicked. Most sources ignore contemporary Muslims, a few treat them pragmatically, and a few demonize them. Section 4 moves into Asia and Africa, lands even fewer English people would know directly. Historians show some sense of different peoples on these continents and their connections to better-known places such as Greece and Rome, but poems and wonder texts often depict inhabitants of these distant places as monstrous. Section 5 discusses imagined lands, places that depart even further from reality with marvelous creatures, people, and animal-human hybrids. Section 6 examines hell, purgatory, and heaven, which are sometimes treated more soberly than the imagined lands of Section 5: early English writers expected everyone to go to at least one of the three destinations. Our Conclusion briefly looks ahead to the later effects of early medieval English ways of seeing the world.

1 England and Scandinavia

Though twenty-first-century novels, films, and video games often imagine the people of the British Isles as ethnically and religiously homogeneous, and these imagined versions of the medieval sometimes influence political movements, the English were never a single ethnicity. Those who would become English combined Celtic and Germanic roots with many other influences, including from Eastern Europe and North Africa. The nation as a political entity occupying stable geographical territory did not yet exist. The fluid alliances and conflicts among the peoples in the British Isles partly reflected the fact that the English themselves lacked a unified identity for much of the pre-Conquest period. They had different relationships of alliance, coexistence, and enmity with their Welsh, Irish and Scottish, and Scandinavian neighbors, and with peoples of mainland Europe.

The British Isles had been a place of immigrants for millennia. Cheddar Man, found in Somerset, lived more than 9,000 years ago. He was a hunter-gatherer with darker skin than was later typical among Northern Europeans. Other waves of immigration likely occurred before Celts from mainland Europe moved into the British Isles by 1000 BCE. All these peoples maintained ties to the mainland, and Romans came repeatedly; Julius Caesar attempted to conquer Britain in 55–54 BCE, and Claudius succeeded in 43 CE. Roman troops occupied England from 43 until around 410; Celts served in the army alongside soldiers from elsewhere in the empire, and Jews were likely present as slaves and/or traders. Bede's geographical introduction to his *Ecclesiastical History of the English People* recalls a more urban, Roman past: Britain enjoyed fame for its twenty-eight cities and many other fortified settlements (Colgrave and Mynors, 1969, I.1). Immigration from a wide area continued even after the Roman withdrawal. Oxygen isotopes in drinking water vary by place and are absorbed in children's teeth, making it possible to identify where a person grew up. They indicate that people buried in British cemeteries from the late Roman era through the Middle Ages originated in many different parts of Europe and around the Mediterranean, including North Africa. Grave goods support these findings (Green, 2016a and 2016b). Ethnicity and cultural identity fluctuated, and peoples intermarried. Different groups within England drew on both internal and mainland European influences to create their own fashions and societies starting in the late fifth century (Fleming, 2010).

Modern people seek linguistic and geographical precision, terms that include every member of a group and no one from outside. We want maps that delineate borders and coordinates to show where land meets water and where polities begin and end. Medieval people knew that affiliations and lands change. People moved, aligned with other cultures, spoke new languages and dialects. Shorelines altered, rivers changed course (Wickham-Crowley, 2006). Those now called "English" did not have a unique name for themselves in the early Middle Ages, nor did they always identify as one people. The English also had complex relationships with Celts, who shared the British Isles with them; and Scandinavians, who sent attackers, settlers, and even kings of England. Thus, "England" and "English" in the early Middle Ages are surprisingly difficult to define.

Early Medieval England

Early medieval English language and culture were shaped by the migration of Germanic peoples in the fifth century. The Old English version of Orosius' *History of the World* describes world geography at length but mentions "Brettannia" only sparingly, and mostly in relation to other places; the text omits some details about the British Isles found in the Latin. There are a few scattered references. Writers more frequently describe smaller areas: fens, ruins, or battlefields; in charters, they list local landmarks, both natural and human-made. The Old English *Chronicle* and Bede's *Ecclesiastical History* are the most extensive sources for information about early medieval England. Both have limitations.

Under King Alfred, manuscripts of the known *Chronicle* up to about 890 were created, copied, and distributed to several different monasteries for continuation; in *Peterborough*, the longest-running version, scribes added material through 1154. The *Chronicle* begins with Julius Caesar's failed attempt to conquer Britain in 60 BCE (actually 55–54). Until 731, the *Chronicle* draws upon Bede's *Ecclesiastical History*, though Bede writes his account in paragraphs spanning decades and centuries, while the *Chronicle* is organized as a sequence of annals. Versions of the *Chronicle* produced at different centers vary in their attentions to different parts of England: the *Peterborough Chronicle* includes detailed entries on that city (in modern Cambridgeshire). The Mercian register (in three manuscripts) gives greater detail and import to Mercia, an independent kingdom until around 900. One manuscript focuses more on traditional West Saxon holdings.

Depictions of early medieval England thus show diverse attitudes. The Isles seem marginal and unimportant in the *Orosius*, while the Cotton World Map (see Introduction) retains their position and enlarges them. The *Chronicle* and Bede focus on England, and when they include events occuring elsewhere, they relate to the British Isles. Britons, a Celtic people, still lived in what would become England, spoke Celtic languages such as Cornish and Welsh, and did not identify as English at all. Felix's eighth-century Latin *Life of St Guthlac* describes the battles against Britons the saint had fought in early life for which he later must make amends, retiring to a monastery and then a hermitage. The paucity of descriptions may result from writers taking their surroundings as a given and from the lack of a sense of unity for England during much of the early medieval period.

Bede does not style himself historian of all the English. The title *Historia ecclesiastica gentis Anglorum* is often translated *Ecclesiastical History of the English People*, but the *Angli* here are not generally the English (Harris, 2003). By *Angli*, Bede usually means Anglians, as distinct from Saxons, Mercians, and Kentish people. For much of the early Middle Ages, "England" had little reality as a concept for most inhabitants. Many called themselves and their language "English," but *Englalond* as a territorial designation hardly appears before the time of Alfred the Great, who ruled from 871 to 899. Moreover, Bede's work is, as the title announces, an "ecclesiastical" history, recounting the conversion of the English to Christianity. Bede was careful to document the events he described, relying on firsthand oral narratives as well as selected written accounts that he believed could be trusted. But Bede is also an evangelist who wants to persuade his audience that England has been thoroughly Christianized. To that end, he depicts pagan religion as unsound and pagan leaders as corrupt. He avoids almost any description of pagan practice. But the survival of pagan place-names as well as the references to pagans in his *History*, in the *Chronicle*, and in homilies suggests that the Christianization of the *Angli* was not as thorough as he would have liked, and of England, not as speedy and complete as later readers have wanted it to be.

Bede opens his *Ecclesiastical History* with the geography of the British Isles. He defines Britain ("Brittania," I.1) as across from Germany, Gaul, and Spain, though with great distance between them. The island is 800 miles long by 200 miles wide, with a coastline of 4,875 miles. The land produces good trees and grape vines. Grazing animals thrive, and many kinds of birds, fish, and eels inhabit the land and waters. People catch seals, dolphins, and whales, use shellfish for pearls and dyes, and bathe in hot springs. Metals and jet abound. Britannia's northern position makes summer days very long and winter days very short in comparison with Italy, Armenia, and Macedonia. Bede lists languages before he names inhabitants: English, British (Welsh), Irish, Pictish, and Latin (I.1), suggesting language, and with it, culture, as the key markers of social ties rather than the occupation of a particular land area. Bede's description enjoyed popularity both in his original Latin and its Old English translation, as well as in a much abbreviated, Old English version that begins three of the *Chronicle* manuscripts.

Bede's narrative starts with Celtic Britons living in what would become England and Wales. Following Gildas and other early historians writing in Latin, Bede criticizes the Britons as lazy people who loved luxury to excess and did not fully live their Christian faith. Unable to defend themselves, they invited Germanic mercenaries from mainland Europe to defend them against attacking Picts (also Celtic; I.15). In Bede's telling, the mercenaries took land from the Britons by force, conquering the survivors and forcing them to flee. More recent scholarship, including archaeological and genetic research, suggests a very different picture: instead of winning by wholesale slaughter and exile, immigrants from Scandinavia and the mainland married Celts while taking powerful positions in society.

By the time Bede wrote, most English had two things in common: language and, at least nominally, religion. Old English had regional dialects, but speakers could generally understand one another. Scribes were only occasionally confused by words or grammatical details from a dialect different from their own, and manuscripts often use forms from multiple dialects. Bede's main theme is conversion, in two forms: conversion to Christianity, and then a turn specifically to Roman Christianity even by most Celtic believers. Some Celts had become Christian during Roman occupation, but their form of Christianity calculated Easter differently than Rome and had other divergent practices. Conflict between Roman and Celtic practices provides one of the central narrative lines for Bede's work and leads to a climax in which most Irish and Scots adopt the Roman calculation of Easter.

Meanwhile, immigrants from mainland Europe followed Germanic pagan gods and practices, and popes dispatched missionaries to convert them. Augustine of Canterbury had been prior of a Roman abbey before Pope Gregory I (the Great) sent him to England to begin converting the English around 597. In 669 and 670, another pope dispatched Theodore and Hadrian to England; their origins lay in Tarsus (in present-day Turkey) and North Africa respectively. Bede passes in silence over the role of Franks, who also played a significant part in conversion. For Bede, non-Christians were *pagani*, "pagans," which originally meant "rustics" in Latin; the Old English renders it *hæðen*, "heathen." *The Ecclesiastical History* presents pagans in Britain as all in the past, though evidence of archaeology and place-names suggests practices and beliefs persisted until at least the start of the Norman period (Estes, 2007).

After the first major wave of Germanic migration, powerful families produced what they called kings, who were rulers of peoples more than of lands: there were kings of the South Saxons, West Saxons, East Angles, Kentish people, Northumbrians, and more (Fleming, 2010, 61–119). The earliest English kingdoms in the fifth and sixth centuries left no contemporary documents. Fleming identifies records of thirteen English kingdoms and royal families in the seventh century but notes that more must have existed: "English kingdoms in this period … were not only numerous, but were in a dizzying state of flux" (Fleming, 2010, 149). The power of different kings and peoples rose and fell; the Mercians were most powerful by the mid-seventh century, only to be supplanted later by the West Saxons (Fleming, 2010, 149). Mercia rose to power again in the eighth century, but as Viking attacks intensified in the ninth, for a time the only English king was Alfred, King of the West Saxons. Meanwhile, smaller kingdoms were swallowed by larger ones or conquered by Danish armies. Kent, near both London and mainland Europe, was a wealthy kingdom in the sixth century but came under the control of Mercians in the mid-eighth century and of West Saxons early in the ninth.

"Vikings" (OE "wicingas") is a catch-all term for raiders, primarily from today's Denmark, Norway, and Sweden. Military attacks and settlements established by Scandinavians had profound effects on English identity and governance. One of the earliest major attacks was the sack in 793 of the Northumbrian monastery in Lindisfarne, a religious and educational center whose devastation foreshadowed worse. Many other raids followed, and once again Scandinavians began to settle in England, especially the north and east. The annal for 866/7 recounts that a "mycel hæðen here" (great heathen army) captured York, replacing the kingdom of the Northumbrians with the Viking-ruled kingdom of York. After repeated attacks, East Anglia fell under the rule of Guthrum in 879, a Viking who accepted baptism with Alfred the Great as his godfather, after the West Saxon king defeated him in battle.

Alfred's biographer Asser styled him the "King of the Anglo-Saxons," as did several charters, but he ruled a West Saxon kingdom much smaller than the future England. His daughter Æthelflæd and son Edward expanded the kingdom south of the Humber; Edward's son Æthelstan conquered Northumbria in 927 to create a single kingdom uniting most English speakers in Britain, along with some who spoke Norse and other languages. The unity of the kingdom had been established, though there were occasionally two competing kings (939–41, 957–9, briefly in 1016, and 1035–7, Keynes, 2014a). After William the Conqueror became king in 1066, texts in English continued to be written and copied into the twelfth century and read in the thirteenth. The impact of Norman French dialect and culture would gradually but irreversibly alter early medieval England, but it would remain one kingdom.

Wales, Scotland, and Ireland

Early medieval geographies and other texts gave little attention to other lands and peoples within what is now called the British Isles. Bede notes that the English share an island with Wales and Scotland. The Old English *Orosius* names neither Wales nor the Welsh, though Ireland appears briefly in the geography (Bately, 1980, 9.10, 19.5, and 19.15), and the main text includes an account of a Roman battle with the British, the Picts, and the Scots (142.11–14). The poem *Widsith* pairs the Irish with the Scots in a single half line (Krapp and Dobbie, 1936, 79) before moving quickly to other peoples in its long list.

Ireland was sometimes called Scotland in early medieval texts, though distinctive terms for Ireland sometimes appear in Latin (*Hibernia*) and Old English (*Igbernia*, *Yrrland*). Bede calls Ireland a land of milk and honey, and a healthier island even than England, where snow never lasts beyond three days, reptiles cannot live, and the environment resists poison. It is a kind of biblical promised land, abundant in produce, fish, and fowl (I.1). The Irish sent monks to Britain and were renowned for learning and piety, and their reputation attracted clerics from Britain to Ireland in turn. Bede calls the Irish "gentem innoxiam et nationi Anglorum semper amicissimam" (a blameless race always most friendly to the English, IV.26), sadly noting the 684 attack on them by King Ecgfrith of Northumbria, viewing as divine punishment his defeat and death at the hands of the Picts the following year. The annal for 891/2 in the *Chronicle* further demonstrates Irish piety with an account of three Irish monks who cast off in a hide boat with only a week's food and no oars or rudder, letting God direct them, and arriving in Cornwall and later at King Alfred's court.

The Irish also had contact with the English mediated by Vikings, who made Dublin a hub and so connected the Irish city to the Scandinavian peninsula and Scandinavian-controlled areas in England. The poem *The Battle of Brunanburh* commemorates the historic battle in 937 when Anlaf, the Viking king of Dublin, led an army with warriors from Scotland, Wales, and Ireland against King Æthelstan of Wessex. Æthelstan's own army of "Engle 7 Seaxe" (Angles and Saxons, Dobbie, 1942, 70) defeated the alliance from abroad, helping secure England's unity and independence for another three generations.

Scots appear surprisingly few times in early medieval English writings. They were generally called *Picti* (Latin) or *Peohtas* (Old English) because "Scot" and "Scotland" were usually used for the Irish and Ireland. In a fascinating but incorrect origin myth, Bede writes that the Picts came to Scotland from Scythia and tried to settle Ireland, but the Irish declared there was no room, recommended northern Britain, and even gave them wives (I.1). The attacks of the Scots, Bede writes, prompted southern Britons to invite mercenaries. Later in the period, Scots rulers and tribes sometimes aligned with the English against Viking and Irish attacks, but they also competed for territory while the boundaries between Scottish and English kingdoms were not yet fixed.

The relationship between England and Wales was complicated and fluid. Offa's Dyke, a long earthwork along the border between England and Wales, was once believed to be an impermeable barrier, but more recent scholarship characterizes it as a modest fortification supported by other installations and with gaps, perhaps including cattle paths. Lindy Brady demonstrates that the Welsh and English living in the borderlands shared a distinctive culture and society (2017). The Old English word *wealh* originally meant "foreigner" but came to mean both "slave" and "Welsh"; *wealhstod* means "translator" or "interpreter." Exeter Book Riddles 12 and 52 describe *wealas* as dark-skinned, perhaps slaves, representing the Welsh as a separate people from the English and revealing ethnic stereotyping (Brady, 2017).[13] Yet Wales also produced the learned Asser, who joined Alfred's court and became Alfred's biographer while still living part of the time in Wales (Stevenson, 1959, chapter 79). Wales takes its place in English imaginations as the home of both a famous scholar and a separate people often described as inferior.

Scandinavia

Though the English people were descended from Germanic and Scandinavian migrations that had established the beginning of English language and culture and divided the late classical from the early medieval period, the relationships between the two peoples remained complicated. From the late eighth century through the end of the early medieval period, Scandinavians staged raids and battles that inflicted on the English severe losses of people, property, and

---

[13] Both Welsh and English owned and traded slaves, and both were held as slaves (Brady, 2017, 82–108).

security. What began as raids turned into settlements. The "great heathen army" began settling in Northumbria, Mercia, and East Anglia in 875. The Treaty of Alfred and Guthrum established territory for each ruler, divided by Watling Street, a route established in antiquity by Britons and paved by Romans during their occupation. English law required the payment of *wergild* (man price) to compensate when one person injured or killed another, stopping the cycle of vengeance; equal payments for Danes and English demonstrated social parity between the two peoples. When Alfred's children and grandchildren united England into one kingdom, they incorporated former Vikings rather than forcing them out. Settlers intermarried and adopted the English language while contributing vocabulary and many place-names. Naturally, Scandinavians who settled in England maintained ties with those in Scandinavia.

Despite these ongoing personal connections, Danish ambitions for English rule continued; the late tenth and early eleventh centuries saw power swing back and forth between English and Scandinavian leaders. Swein Forkbeard, the king of Denmark from the late 980s until 1014, raided England in the 990s and conquered it in 1013, but he remained king of England only for some months. The English king, Æthelred II, fled with his family to Normandy in 1013, returned on Swein's death, and resumed his rule. Swein's son Cnut invaded in 1015 and, when Æthelred died in 1016, Cnut became the king of England, ruling for almost twenty years. Cnut also became the ruler of Denmark and parts of Norway and Sweden, "presid[ing] over a veritable 'North Sea empire'" (Keynes, 2014b, 111). After Cnut's death in 1035, Æthelred's son Alfred returned from Normandy to rule, but he was killed and Cnut's sons succeeded him. In 1042, Edward the Confessor succeeded the second son, putting a descendant of Alfred back on the throne until 1066.

"Scandinavia" and "Scandinavian" are modern words. Early English writers frequently used a few catch-all terms for people from what we would now call Denmark, Sweden, and Norway; like England, the Scandinavian countries were defined and united later. While *Dene* and *Dani* might specifically designate Danes, they sometimes also stood more broadly for Scandinavians. *Norðmen* could describe Norwegians or be used for Northerners in any context. *Chronicle* annalists often do not distinguish whether a specific group of raiders came from Denmark, Norway, Sweden, or farther afield, and many war bands probably included warriors from various places.

Sometimes, though, English writers made a point to distinguish among different regions and peoples. The Old English *Orosius* specifies Danes and Denmark in passages translated from Latin as well as in two added accounts. Ohthere's travelogue, addressed to King Alfred, uses "Northmen" as a blanket term but also distinguishes Sweden (*Sweoland*, 15.33) from Norway (*Norðweg*, 16.9) and Denmark (*Dene*, 16.15, *Denamearc* 16.16 and 20). Wulfstan lists individual areas as belonging to "Denemearcan" (16.25) and "Sweon" (Swedes, 16.27).[14] *Beowulf*, though a largely fictional tale of monsters and heroes, also memorializes some aspects of Scandinavian culture: the poem clearly differentiates *Dene* or *Scyldinga* (sons of Scyld) from *Geatas* and Swedes (*Scilfingas* or *Sweona*).[15] The *Beowulf* poet also distinguishes *Suðdene* from other Danish peoples. Writers' purposes affected their choices: alliances and enmities between peoples are central to *Beowulf*, so distinguishing them matters.

Other English terms for Scandinavians identify them by activities. *Wicing* (Viking) names sea raiders, often but not always Scandinavian. Words for sailors (*flotman, sæman*) were occasionally used similarly. Homilists and annalists often emphasized religion over ethnicity. In *Saint Edmund*, Ælfric calls the attacking army both Danish (26) and "heathen," which with half a dozen occurrences in this life alone outnumbers geographical references (Clayton and Mullins 2019, vol. 3, 186–205). Wulfstan, along with other homilists and chroniclers, similarly dubs Scandinavians *hæðen*, even though many were Christian. "Danes" and "heathens" often appear interchangeably in religious and historical sources that present them as threats to both life and faith.

The distance between England and Scandinavia seems literally and figuratively small. In the *Orosius*, Ohthere says that he lives northmost of all Northmen (13.29–30), in Halgoland (modern Halogaland) with only wasteland and scattered small groups of Finns to his north. His narrative focuses primarily on this distant land, touching more briefly on his travels in *Sciringesheal* (probably Kaupang, Norway), Ireland, Jutland, Denmark, and Germany. Similarly, Wulfstan tells of his travels through the Baltic. Whoever recorded these originally oral accounts seems fascinated by travel, not from Norway or Denmark to England, but among places outside England – the more distant, the better. Ohthere may have known English or used an interpreter (Bately, 1980, lxxi–ii). These and other encounters between Old English and Old Norse speakers do not mention translators; the early medieval forms of these languages were closer than their modern forms and so were likely mutually intelligible.

Even when Vikings were enemies, some early English writers felt a kinship to Scandinavians. The West Saxon Genealogy, which traces the lineage of King Alfred the Great, appears in three manuscripts. Though Alfred fought Viking attackers throughout his reign, this text from the 890s recorded one of Alfred's forebears as descended from Woden, Geat, Heremod, and Beaw or Beow – Scandinavian names. Heremod and Beow also appear in *Beowulf*. Two of the

---

[14] Some scholars believe Wulfstan was a foreign traveler like Ohthere, others that he was an English trader or a missionary to Baltic peoples.

[15] What "Geats" meant to the early English is murky; see Valtonen, 2008, especially 206.

manuscripts add "Sceafing," indicating that one Bedwig is the son of Sceaf – as is *Beowulf*'s Scyld.

Beowulf, written in English but with no English characters, provides our most detailed early medieval English perspective on Scandinavians. The only surviving copy was written down about 1000, but its date of composition is controversial for many reasons, not least because some scholars find it hard to imagine English audiences enjoying the tale of a Geat defending first Danes and then his own tribe when Scandinavians had inflicted great harm on the English since 793. Its named characters are almost all elite warriors who raid other settlements and defend their own from raids. Several named high-status women form alliances by marriage as "peace-weavers." The characters live in small settlements centered on halls where they gather, as in many early English settlements (Gardiner, 2011; Hamerow, 2011). In *Beowulf*, a *scop* (pronounced *shope*) sings stories of creation (90–8), battles, revenge, and loss (1063–1159) in the hall. The shorter poems *Deor* and *Widsith* also depict *scopas*. The early medieval English and Scandinavian peoples shared the cultural touchstones of *scop*, hall, and warrior lifestyle.

Conclusion

As detailed in this section, England did not become a unified land with a set name until the tenth century. Its people used multiple names, sometimes identifying with smaller groups (Saxons, Angles) and sometimes with the larger *Angelcyn* (English people). In histories, chronicles, charters, homilies, and poetry, a wide range of texts show English interest in the land they inhabit and their near neighbors. Place and identity mattered, but their conceptions of borders and belonging were more fluid than many of ours today. They recognized that affiliations shifted due to politics and nature, and people could change their allegiances or identify with more than one group simultaneously.

2 Mainland Europe

England had close ties to Europe beyond Scandinavia, particularly with the Franks and Rome. Never homogeneous nor wholly insular, early medieval English writers emphasized their participation in wide economic and religious networks. The Old English *Orosius* attests detailed (if not always accurate) early English knowledge of European geography. Travelers' accounts and letters to and from Boniface included in his mission, chronicles, and histories show clergy and courtiers moving between England and mainland Europe, especially among the lands that would become France, the Low Countries, Germany, and Italy. English interests extended beyond these well-traveled paths to Byzantium, the Baltic, and the Iberian Peninsula, as well as to Jerusalem and the eastern Mediterranean (see Section 3). The British Isles in turn welcomed many from mainland Europe.

English writers showed surprisingly little interest in landscapes or buildings elsewhere in Europe, but they wrote a great deal about the peoples. Just as those who would later be called "English" went by varied names, so did other European peoples. People's allegiances and nomenclatures shifted and lands changed hands as groups and leaders competed for power and resources. This section does not cover the many names and divisions fully, but it gives an overview of how the early medieval English conceived of parts of mainland Europe.

Franks and Francia

In antiquity, much of what is now France was called Gaul and its people were known as Gauls. Bede and other early medieval writers used that terminology, but Bede also referred to Franks (*Franci*), a term later English writers preferred and that is used here. In early histories, Franks appear as members of the Roman Empire. Bede links Gaul to Britain by writing that Constantius Chlorus governed Gaul and Spain until his death in Britain, and that his son Constantine, who later gained renown as the first Christian emperor, succeeded him while himself in Britain (I.8). Contacts between Britain and the Franks forged in Roman times persisted or were renewed after Germanic peoples moved to England, and these connections were substantial throughout the early medieval English period. Though the term "insular" suggests a strong separation between England and mainland Europe, in the early medieval period, as later, this was seldom the case: the English Channel served more as a transportation hub than a barrier.

In sixth- and seventh-century Kent and the upper Thames valley, the presence of Frankish grave goods indicates regular trade and perhaps intermarriage (Fleming, 2010). Though Bede focuses on missionaries coming directly from Rome, other evidence shows that Franks had major religious influence. King Æthelbert of Kent (d. 616) was married to a Frankish Christian, Bertha, before his conversion; she "apparently established St Martin's in a dilapidated Roman building, which she had shored up and remodeled to look like a Frankish church" (Fleming, 2010, 186). Augustine of Canterbury brought Franks as translators on his mission from Rome.[16] Aristocratic men and women went to mainland Europe to become monks and nuns among the Franks shortly after conversion, also suggesting preexisting ties: for example, Eorcengota, daughter

---

[16] Apparently their Franconian language resembled the Kentish dialect at the time (Colgrave and Mynors, 1969, 73n4).

of Eadbald, the king of Kent (616–40), entered a monastery at Brie. Abbess Hild (ca. 614–80) planned to take the veil in mainland Europe but was instead persuaded to found and direct houses in England.

Frankish and English families maintained ties for political and personal reasons, which kept their languages and cultures in conversation. After the death of King Edwin of Northumbria in 633, his widow, Queen Æthelburh, sent her son and grandson, both small children but potential claimants to the throne, to King Dagobert in Francia in order to protect them from King Oswald. Both died young. Had they lived, they might have returned to England with Frankish customs and learning, as did Sigeberht, a king of the East Angles, who was baptized and educated in exile in Francia. After returning to East Anglia around 630, Sigeberht established a school based on those in Francia. In the eighth century, Ecgberht spent years in exile in Francia before becoming the king of the West Saxons in 802. Alcuin, on the other hand, grew up and was ordained a deacon in York and joined Charlemagne's court in the early 780s. He visited York again in the early 790s and wrote a poem commemorating its library as it had been before the Viking attack. Alcuin synthesized English and Frankish learning, becoming highly influential in both mainland Europe and England.

Royal families maintained cultural, linguistic, and educational ties in the ninth century. King Ecgberht of Wessex spent at least three years in exile in Francia; his son Æthelwulf succeeded him as the king of Wessex and married thirteen-year-old Judith, daughter of King Charles the Bald of West Francia. Upon Æthelwulf's death in 858, after only two years of marriage, his son Æthelbald married Judith, which both solidified Æthelbald's claim to the throne (at this time, the eldest son did not always succeed his father as king) and strengthened ties to the Frankish royal family. When Æthelbald died in 860, Judith was only seventeen and had no children; she returned home to her father before marrying Baldwin of Flanders over her father's objections. After Alfred, Æthelwulf's youngest son, eventually came to the throne, he brought to his court mainland European scholars, including Grimbald of Saint-Bertin.

In the next generation, a son of Judith and Baldwin married Ælfthryth, daughter of King Alfred. Eadgifu of Wessex, Alfred's granddaughter, married King Charles III of West Francia. After Charles lost the Battle of Soissons in 923 and then his crown, Eadgifu took her young son Louis back home to Wessex; at the age of fifteen, he succeeded to the throne his father had held. As King Louis IV, he was also called Louis *d'Outremer* (from overseas). Louis probably brought back with him an English coronation rite that itself had borrowed from earlier Frankish rites.

The tenth century saw continued mutual influence. Many of the Frankish transplants composed works in Latin for English instruction. The Benedictine

Reform that began in England in the mid-tenth century drew heavily on what is now France for texts, liturgical practices, and personnel. Several prominent (and doubtless many lesser known) Frankish clerics went to England as teachers and writers: Abbo of Fleury taught at Ramsey in the mid-980s; around the same time, Frithegod taught at Canterbury and composed Latin poetry while Lantfred, who had migrated from Fleury to take up monastic life in Winchester, wrote rhyming Latin prose. A later wave of Frankish clergy living in England in the mid-eleventh century included Folcard of Saint-Bertin, who wrote several Latin lives and was the abbot of Thorney Abbey after the Conquest; and Goscelin of Saint-Bertin, secretary to the Bishop of Sherborne and Wilton Abbey's chaplain. Goscelin wrote many Latin lives and miracle stories as well as the *Liber confortatorius* (*Book of Reassurance*) (ca. 1083), addressed to Eve, a young English woman who left Wilton for anchoritic life in France. While the English have sometimes imagined themselves isolated from outside cultural influences, this was certainly not the case in the early Middle Ages or during Norman rule.

Normans and the Norman Conquest

Both family and clerical connections between England and Francia intensified in the eleventh century. Northern France itself had changed: much as they had done in England, so in France the Vikings settled, intermarried, and became known as Normans; their language was called Norman or Norman French. A brief look at the lives of King Edward, Earl Godwine, and their families shows the complexity of English connections (and the artificiality, however useful, of this Element's organization). King Edward the Confessor, born between 1003 and 1005, lived in Normandy from 1013 to 1041, during a period when England was mostly ruled by Danish kings. Then his half-brother, King Harthacnut of England, recalled him to be joint king, and Edward became sole king at Harthacnut's death in 1042. As king, Edward selected a Norman friend as the archbishop of Canterbury, the highest religious post in England.[17] Others among Edward's Norman favorites gained power in England and began building castles there.

The powerful Earl Godwine presented a challenge to King Edward. Godwine himself probably had Scandinavian heritage and married into King Cnut's family. Though he seems to have betrayed Edward's brother Alfred, the king found

---

[17] This friend, Robert of Jumièges, would later flee England for his previous monastery. There, he donated a lavishly illuminated English manuscript now known as the Missal of Robert of Jumièges, leaving an enduring example of Winchester's manuscript art in Normandy. For images, see Thijs Porck (December 25, 2017) Category Archives: Missal of Robert of Jumièges, *Thijs Porck*, https://thijsporck.com/category/manuscripts/missal-of-robert-of-jumieges.

Godwine too powerful to oppose and married his daughter Edith in 1045. When a group of Normans had a deadly brawl with Englishmen in Dover in 1051, King Edward ordered Godwine to move against the English; he refused. Edward then charged Godwine with Alfred's murder and repudiated Edith. Godwine and his family fled to Bruges and Ireland but returned the following year and, with armed support from Ireland and Normandy, appeared at King Edward's council. Godwine's property and position were restored and Edward took Edith back as his wife.

According to some sources, Godwine's son Harold traveled to Normandy around 1064 and was shipwrecked and captured by a Norman magnate but freed by William, Duke of Normandy. After fighting for William in a military campaign in Brittany, where some sources say he relayed a promise from Edward that William would succeed him as king and added his own, Harold returned to England before Edward's death early in 1066. Some documents claim that Edward designated Harold his successor from his deathbed. The aristocracy affirmed the choice and the archbishop of York anointed Harold king with unprecedented haste a mere day after Edward's death. Later that year, an army from Norway sought to conquer England before Harold could fully solidify his grip. Harold led the English army to victory against this invasion at Stamford Bridge in northern England, but William set sail from Normandy and claimed the throne supposedly promised him by Kings Edward and Harold. The exhausted English army made a strong showing in southern England, but with the deaths of King Harold and two of his brothers, they lost to the Normans. William became William I, the Conqueror, King of England, and the Normans became the domin-ant political and religious force in England. English noblemen were killed or exiled. England became even more multilingual and multicultural, underscoring that England has never been isolated or independent from other lands and peoples.

Frisia and Germania

Today's maps draw clear boundaries between France, Germany, and the Low Countries; the early medieval situation was more complex and less settled. At times, Frisians recognized the authority of Frankish kings; at other times, Frisia was independent. Old English documentary texts contain many more references to Franks and Francia (*Francland*, *Francrice*, or *France*) than to Friesland and Frisians, though the poetic corpus has roughly equal numbers of references. The *Beowulf* poet uses the two terms as synonyms (1207–10, 2910) but distin-guishes among the east Frankish *Gifðas*, *Hetware*, and *Wylfingas*. The short Old English poem *Widsith*'s narrator, Widsith (Wide Travel), lists many indi-viduals and peoples he has visited and some historical events. Germanic tribes and leaders feature prominently, mixed with many others. Frisians and Franks are distinguished in a brief mention in the line, "Mid Froncum ic wæs ond mid Frysum ond mid Frumtingum" (I was with Franks and with Frisians and with Frumtingans, Krapp and Dobbie, 1936, 68). The poet names Germanic tribes (Franks, Lombards, and Myrgingas) alongside biblical peoples (Israelites and Assyrians) without distinguishing them in longevity or fame. We cannot tell whether readers then would have recognized the Myrgingas and other tribes now obscure, or whether the poem reflects contemporary uncertainties about peoples and their places and times. In sources from antique Latin to twenty-first-century history books, the battle at which Constantine adopted Christianity takes place in Rome. In the Old English poem *Elene*, however, Constantine and the Romans fight "Huna leode ond Hreðgotan ... Francan ond Hugas" (Huns and Goths ... Franks and Hugas, Krapp, 1932, 20, 21a) at the Danube, giving Germanic tribes a key, if unwitting, role in catalyzing the conversion.[18]

While much of Francia became Christian relatively early, Frisia did not. Frisians migrated to England around the fifth century along with Saxons, Angles, and Jutes. Their language remained close to Old English, facilitating English missions there. Willibrord (657/8–739) led a band of a dozen missionaries to mainland Europe. He went first to the Frankish king, Pippin II, who directed him to Frisia and offered support, protection, and land. The pope named him the archbishop to the Frisians. He ran into many difficulties but founded a diocese in Utrecht and a monastery at Echternach.

English peoples including West Saxons, East Saxons, and South Saxons shared names and a sense of heritage with mainland Saxons and other groups, whom they sought to convert. Boniface (originally named Wynfrith) (ca. 675–754) made an unsuccessful expedition to Frisia before a commission from Pope Gregory II took him through many Frankish areas, mostly in what is now Germany. He founded several monasteries and bishoprics and was martyred with fifty-two others in what became the Netherlands. Berhtgyth, an English nun and missionary to Thuringia, wrote letters and poetry; according to a later biography of Boniface, Berthgyth's mother, Cynehild, had traveled to mainland Europe as well (Maude, 2017).[19] Leoba too originally hailed from England. Boniface gave her special permission to visit Fulda, where no other women were allowed (Talbot, 1954, 223), and asked that she be buried with him (she was not, 222 and 224). Boniface corresponded with colleagues in England, including the abbesses Eadburh of Thanet and Bugga of Kent, from whom he requested manuscripts, an indicator of the high quality of women's scribal

---

[18] Fulk, Bjork, and Niles, 2008, 470, follow Klaeber in glossing "Hugas" as another name for Franks.

[19] Thanks to Nicole Songstad for her help here and with the letters of Bugga.

products. The striking number of women in Boniface's circle reflects the higher status of women in early medieval England than in mainland Europe or after the Norman Conquest: high-status English women, lay or clerical, owned and bequeathed property, ruled monastic houses, and advised secular leaders.

The importance of Wealhtheow and Thryth/Modthryth in *Beowulf*, and the role of the "peace-weaver" (*freoðuwebbe*), have been ignored or underestimated in much scholarship. Foreshadowing of the burning of Heorot has been taken to point to Wealhtheow's failure to make peace, without recognizing the decades of truce that she *did* successfully mediate, even during the predations of Grendel. Thryth appears first as cruel, having men killed simply for looking at her, but upon marrying Offa she becomes a proper queen.[20] Most scholars identify *Beowulf*'s Offa with a mainland Germanic king of that name, but the name could also evoke the eighth-century Mercian king Offa, possibly adding a reference closer to home for English audiences of this poem set in mainland Europe.

Italy

The early English also had great interest in Romans and other Italians – so much that Nicholas Howe described their conception of Europe as "an intellectual and spiritual *patria* [homeland] that had Rome as its capital" (2004, 148). Rome was the actual capital of the empire, including the British Isles, from Emperor Claudius' conquest of Britain in 46 CE until Rome's withdrawal of its troops in 410. Bede's *Ecclesiastical History* and all manuscripts of the *Chronicle* refer to significant events from Rome. The Roman Empire is as central to the Old English *Orosius* as it was to its Latin source.

As the home of popes, Rome remained a spiritual capital long after secular Italian empires had declined (Howe, 2008, 101–24). Missionaries left Rome for England, as we have seen; in turn, religious men and women such as Boniface (ca. 675–754) went to Rome for instructions, blessings, and contemplation. Boniface wrote to Abbess Bugga in Kent, encouraging her to make a pilgrimage to Rome, where their friend Wiethburga went (Ferrante et al., 2014). A nun, Hygeburg, recorded the best-documented early English pilgrimage to Jerusalem and its environs. Hygeburg was an English transplant to the Thuringian double monastery of Heidenheim; her *Hodoeporicon* (*Traveler's Book*, ca. 723–4) recounts the pilgrimage of her countryman Willibald from his oral account (Lapidge, 2014, 251). Katharine Scarfe Beckett cautions that no evidence shows the text reached medieval England (2003, 44). Yet the choices

---

[20] For the character's name, see Fulk, Bjork, and Niles, 2008, note on 1931f. For more on early English ideas of peaceweaving women, see Klein, 2006.

Willibald made in his destinations and recollections, and Hygeburg in crafting a narrative from them, reflect individual perspectives and broader conceptions shaped by English culture that join textual authority to personal experience. The *Hodoeporicon* lists the cities Willibald passed through on his way to and from Jerusalem, including a number in Italy; his father died at Luca and was interred there. Etna and Vulcano, a volcanic island, stand out in Hygeburg's work (Holder-Egger, 1887, 93.8–10 and 101.30–102.2; cf. Talbot, 1954, 160 and 171), showing unusual attention to landscape, which features relatively little in her account and many others. It may have held special interest because Willibald expects Vulcano to offer a vicarious experience of hell. Etna also appears in the Old English *Boethius* and its Meters and the *Orosius*, showing continued interest in the site.

In the 850s, King Æthelwulf of Wessex took his young son, the future Alfred the Great, to Rome; Alfred's biographer Asser suggests that his memories of travel to Rome were formative. Rome hosted permanent settlers from England too, who had such a presence that their area became known as the *burh*, Old English for fortification or town; Italians still call it the *Borgo*.[21] The *Dialogues* of Gregory the Great, a long series of miracle stories set in Italian cities from the sixth century, were translated into Old English, possibly at Alfred's direction. Many other saints' lives in both Latin and Old English are set explicitly in Italy. Curiously, the texts tend to give names but not to describe buildings or landscapes, though they must have struck English visitors as different from their own: stone buildings were common in Italy but rare in England.

Archbishop Sigeric of Canterbury visited Rome in 990, staying in the "Schola Anglorum" (Ortenburg, 1990, 204–6) established for English visitors. In his "Itinerary," Sigeric catalogues several churches he visited in the city and then lists the eighty cities, villages, and hospices where he stopped on his way overland back to England. From Italy, where he stayed in Vercelli, he crossed the passes of Switzerland into France, finally crossing the English Channel near Calais (Ortenburg, 1990, 228–44). Someone left the Vercelli Book, a manuscript of Old English religious poems and prose homilies, in the city of Vercelli, probably on their way to or from Rome. In the early twelfth century, William of Malmesbury incorporated another eighth-century guide by a pilgrim from Malmesbury to forty churches in Rome into his *Gesta Regum* (*Deeds of Kings*). Various documents show that throughout the early medieval period, the English felt that they belonged to a wide community centered in Rome.

---

[21] Howe, 2008, 101–3.

Eastern Europe

Byzantium, though further afield, was also considered part of the broader community with which the English affiliated themselves and that engaged their imaginations. Theodore of Canterbury, born and raised in West Asia, received an extensive education in the Byzantine Empire before moving to Rome and later becoming the archbishop of Canterbury in 669. Theodore and his companion Hadrian, an African (see Section 4), founded a school at Canterbury that produced biblical commentaries that had a major impact on early medieval English religion and scholarship. Willibald and his companions (as detailed by Hygeburg) traveled through Greece on the way to Palestine, stopping at Syracuse before sailing past the city of Corinth and the islands of Chios and Samos. They began their tour of holy sites in Greece with the postbiblical tomb of the Seven Sleepers (Holder-Egger, 1887, 93.16; trans. Talbot, 1954, 160). This legend tells of seven young Christians entombed in a cave as martyrs, but instead of dying, they sleep for almost four centuries before they awake to proclaim true Christianity to an empire that had converted but was beset by heresy. The tomb was popular in England: the story appears in multiple Latin and Old English texts, though most extant versions are later.[22] They later saw two stylites – ascetics living atop pillars – in Miletus (Talbot, 1954, 160–1). On their return, they visited Constantinople and Nicaea, and Hygeburg briefly explains these cities' importance in early Christian history (Talbot, 1954, 171). In the late tenth century, Bishop Æthelwold's household included an exiled Greek bishop, Nikephorus, known in English as Sigewold; his presence may have contributed to the popularity of Greek-derived vocabulary during Æthelwold's episcopacy (Lapidge, 2002, 386–99). The Greek Constantinus, who may have been a bishop, spent years at Malmesbury in the early eleventh century (Lapidge, 2002, 379–86). Both laity and clergy went on pilgrimages that took them to or through Constantinople. Archaeological and manuscript evidence shows the movement of objects from Byzantium to England from the earliest times through the Norman Conquest (Lapidge, 2002, 364–5).

Writers forged literary connections as well. Though Ælfric generally shows even less interest in place than other Old English writers, his *Saint Basil* transports readers from Basil's ordination as a deacon at Antioch to his later bishopric in Cappadocia and the burial of his body in Caesarea. In *The Letter of Alexander to Aristotle*, an Old English version of an originally Greek wonder text through Latin, the Greek emperor describes himself as a Macedonian in the first sentence, and he writes back home to his teacher, Aristotle, about his

---

[22] See Kramer, Magennis, and Norris, 2020, 587–651, for one anonymous version; see also their introduction, xxxiii–xxxiv, for other versions and references, including references in six Old English charms and a brief retelling by Ælfric.

expedition to India and the wonders he finds (see Section 5). The Old English *Orosius* maintains distinctions among Athenians, Macedonians, Spartans, and residents of other Greek city-states. *Widsith* also names Alexander and the Greeks. *Elene* recounts that Emperor Constantine's mother, Helen, leads (*lædan*, 241) a ship of warriors from Rome to Jerusalem. Following early medieval practice, they do not sail straight across the Mediterranean but hug the coast and make landfall in Greece. The cheerful, memorable voyage, led by a woman, receives quite a long description (225–75; 51 of 1,321 lines). The place of Greece in texts from histories and saints' lives to poetry both relied on and reinforced audiences' sense of where it was and how it connected to religious and political history.

More distant parts of Eastern Europe appear in extant accounts as well. The most detailed narrative is Wulfstan's voyage, a companion to Ohthere's (see Section 1). Wulfstan recounts sailing from Hedeby, in what is now Denmark, east to Poland, where he repeatedly names the Vistula River and identifies Truso as a trading center. He describes the funeral customs of the Ests, an eastern Germanic or Baltic people. They hold five or six days of celebration after a man dies, then divide his belongings, with the largest portion going to the fastest horse and rider, the next largest to the second, and so on. The hoards of pre-Conquest English coins found in Poland and Russia suggest more contact than extant writings reveal.

Iberia

The Iberian Peninsula occupies an ambiguous place in English geography. Bede describes Britain as opposite Germany, Gaul, and Spain, and southern Ireland as opposite the northern part of Spain (Colgrave and Mynors, 1969, I.1). Obviously, sailors must go a good deal south from either Ireland or Britain to reach Spain, but Bede's geography speaks to a sense of closeness stronger than a modern map would show. The Cotton World Map (Figure 2) similarly compresses the Bay of Biscay to show Spain much closer to Cornwall than it should be. The Iberian Peninsula was an important part of the late Roman Empire; Paulus Orosius probably came from there. Orosius' *History* and the Old English version recount many Roman battles in Iberia, including against Hannibal. The Visigoths, a Germanic group that settled parts of Spain in the fifth century, ruled for approximately 300 years. Gregory the Great's *Dialogues* and its Old English translation tell the story of the Visigothic King Leuvigild and his son Ermengild (died 585). Leuvigild followed the teachings of Arius, whose beliefs the Roman Church considered heretical. With Arius' help, he sought to raise his son as an Arian, but Bishop Leander persuaded Ermengild to follow

Roman teachings. Ermengild was subsequently martyred (Hecht, 1900–7, III.31). Ælfric identifies St. Vincent and St. Laurence as Spanish, and he recounts missionary work and miracles in Spain in multiple homilies and lives.

Few early medieval English people would have met a Muslim, so their ideas about Islam were drawn from textual sources, and writers characterized Spanish Muslims as a religious threat. Bede describes their attacks as "grauissima ... lues Gallias misera caede uastabat" (a most terrible calamity [that] devastated Gaul with deplorable slaughter) in 729, and he adds they were punished soon after (V.23, though it is unclear what punishment he means; see 557n5). Boniface wrote to King Æthelbald around 746–7 about the king's sexual sins, arguing that God had allowed Muslims to attack Spain, Provence, and Burgundy because of rulers' sexual misconduct (Talbot, 1954, 124); he also tells Bugga that Wiethburga says she should not travel until Muslim raids against Rome have subsided (Ferrante et al., 2014). The *Peterborough Chronicle* says that Charlemagne entered Spain, destroyed the cities of Pamplona and Saragossa, and conquered the Muslims (Irvine, 2004, 778).[23] While early English writers saw themselves as part of a community that ranged widely across Europe, North Africa, and East Asia, they emphatically believed that Jews and Muslims were not part of that community. In their relatively sparse comments about Spain, early English writers see themselves in continuity with Roman civilization and Christian piety, but also in opposition to early Christian heretics and contemporary Muslims.

Conclusion

Though England occupied a corner of world maps, religious, familial, commercial, and military networks bound it to many areas throughout mainland Europe. Francia, Rome, and Byzantium were very important to the people of England throughout the early medieval period (and beyond). Individuals moved because of marriage, advancement, or exile. Latin provided a contact language through much of Europe and elsewhere. English travelers or visitors to England found ways to communicate. Popes sent instructions and personnel while English people made pilgrimages and other journeys and wrote about them. These writers and thinkers did not think of themselves as insular but considered themselves part of a Christian community that spanned Western and Central Europe, North Africa, and East Asia. Within this worldview, place of origin and color of skin mattered little, but religion did: English writers absolutely did not consider Muslims or Jews part of their community.

---

[23] The *Chronicle* here uses the derogatory term "Saracen" for Muslims; see Scarfe Beckett, 2003, 94–5, and Section 3, for the usage and why we avoid it.

3 Jerusalem and Its Environs

Europe, Asia, and Africa meet around Jerusalem, located at the center of early medieval maps and sometimes described as the center of the world. The "loca sancta" or "holy lands," as people in early medieval England called Jerusalem and places surrounding it, were of crucial importance in the Christian imagination, along with the peoples who lived there. We borrow the term "holy lands" here to illuminate an area in Asia set apart by early medieval writers. Jerusalem and its environs are depicted in adaptations of biblical narratives, saints' lives, and homilies. *Judith*, *Exodus*, and *Daniel* follow Christological readings of the "Old Testament" – Hebrew scriptures appropriated by early Christians – that distinguish figures like Judith and Daniel, defined as "Hebrews" who anticipate Christianity, from "Jews" as the ancestors of Jews in the Christian Bible who are later blamed for killing Jesus. Poems based on Latin lives of saints such as *Elene* and *Juliana* draw clear distinctions among Hebrews, Jews, pagans, and Christians. Pilgrimage accounts describe holy places traversed by Christians and nearly empty of Jews, though occupied by Muslims. Muslims in turn appear as a threat spreading across lands holy to Christians. Latin provided English speakers a common language with religious and educated Christians in other lands, allowing travelers to share stories and bring them back for English consumption.

Jews before Christianity

In adopting the Hebrew Bible as their Old Testament, Christians appropriated holy Jewish figures as their own, as is evident in some Old English biblical poems. The Junius manuscript begins with a poetic adaptation of the start of Genesis through the death of Abraham. *Exodus*, next, narrates the portion of the biblical book of Exodus in which the Jews flee the Egyptians by crossing the Red Sea, with embedded narratives of the flood and of Abraham's journey to sacrifice Isaac. *Daniel* follows, and then a poem titled *Christ and Satan*. The codex as a whole provides a Christological reading of the Old Testament in miniature, from Creation to what the *Daniel*-poet imagines as the Jews' fall into sin, followed by the arrival in the final poem of Jesus as savior.

The Old English *Daniel* represents portions of chapters 1 through 5 of the biblical book (Krapp, 1931, xxxi). It begins by describing the Jews' descent into sin in a passage that may be transposed from Daniel 9:4–17, which suggests that Antiochus' persecutions result from Israelites' sins. *Daniel* opens, "Gefrægn ic Hebreos eadge lifgean / in Hierusalem" (I have heard of Hebrews living prosperously in Jerusalem, 1–2a). Here, "Hebrews" is used, as almost always in Old English poetry, to describe devout Jews before the advent of Christianity. A few lines later, however, the poem turns to a lengthy description of Jewish perfidy, saying "Israhela cyn" (Israelite people, 24) had power "oðþæt hie wlenco anwod æt winþege / deofoldædum, druncne geðohtas" (until at their wine-banquets, pride invaded them with devilish deeds and drunken thoughts, 17–18). The poem adds that the people "in gedwolan hweorfan" (turned to heresy, 22) and "curon deofles cræft" (chose the devil's deceits, 32). "Israelites" is a generally neutral term for the Jewish people, also used of Moses and his people as they flee Pharaoh in the Old English *Exodus,* but here used in contrast to "Hebrews."

In the poem, Nebuchadnezzar seeks out the wisest Jews: Hananiah, Mishael, and Azariah (also known as Shadrach, Meschach, and Abednego). Later, he crafts a gold statue and demands that the Jews worship it, but the three men refuse to do so. Nebuchadnezzar orders them bound and thrown into a furnace, where an angel protects them from harm while they pray.[24] The three men are called "Ebrea" (Hebrews, 256), and given a Christian prayer in which they call upon "fæder ælmihtig, / soð sunu metodes, sawla nergend, / and þec, halig gast" (Father almighty, true son of God, savior of souls, and you, holy spirit, 401b–403). *Daniel* contrasts "Hebrews" as proto-Christians with "Israelites" as ancestors of contemporary Jews, seen as wicked and faithless. For the Christian writers of the Junius poems, the pre-Christian Israelites who lived in and around Jerusalem serve a Christian narrative of a people once chosen by God but later superseded by Christians, who imagine themselves as the true inheritors of Jewish scripture.

The poetic adaptation of Judith is based on chapters 12 through 15 of the biblical text.[25] In the biblical narrative preceding the surviving poem, a general, Holofernes, has subjugated everyone to the rule of Nebuchadnezzar; only "filii Israhel qui habitabant in terra Iudaeae" (the sons of Israel who live in the land of Judea, Dobbie, 1953, Jud. 4:1) refuse to surrender. Holofernes besieges the city. Judith, a wealthy and devout widow, dons her best clothing and jewels, and God gives her incomparable beauty. Taking one servant with her, she leaves the city and goes to Holofernes' camp, where she tells the guard that she will share the Hebrews' secrets with Holofernes. Holofernes sees her and "captus est in suis oculis" (is captured in his eyes, Jud. 10:17). She tells Holofernes that God is angry with her people and she will show him how to capture her city without bloodshed. He grants her permission to leave the city each night after dark to pray.

As it survives, Judith's narrative begins on her fourth night in the encampment, when Holofernes throws a riotous feast and goads his men to drink until

---

[24] Scheil, 2016, includes extensive sections on early medieval English ideas of Babylon and treats *Daniel* in depth on 67–81.

[25] The poem is missing its opening lines. Mark Griffith surveys other scholarship and argues from the elimination of many characters and rearrangement of details that relatively few poetic lines have been lost (1997, 1–4 and 47–61).

they lie swooning, "swylce hie wæron deaðe geslegene" (as if they had been slain to the death, 41b). He orders Judith brought to his tent, where he plans to rape her. Instead, "se rica" (the mighty one, 68) falls onto his bed, so drunk that "he nyste ræda nanne / on gewitlocan" (he knew no sense in his mind, 68–9). "Rica," meaning one who is strong, mighty, powerful, is used here with irony to denote Holofernes just in the moment that he collapses from too much drinking.

The poem makes Judith a proto-Christian "Hebrew." Judith draws Holofernes' sword and prays. The Old English poet transforms her biblical prayer to "Lord God of Israel" (13:8) into Christian prayer like that given the three youths in *Daniel*, addressed to "frymða god ond frofre gæst, / bearn alwaldan … ðrynesse ðrym" (God of creation and holy spirit, son of God … glory of the Trinity, 83–5). The Jewish notion of a singular undivided God directly contrasts with unity in Trinity, a mystery of the Christian faith.

Holofernes is called "þone hæðenan hund" (the heathen dog, 110) in the moment before Judith cuts off Holofernes' head and it rolls across the floor. The alliteration highlights Holofernes' inferior status through both the metaphorical identification with an animal and the contrast in his religious affiliation with that of Hebrews-as-proto-Christians. Immediately after this, he is rendered an object, divided into two parts. Judith's servant packs the head in their food bag and they leave the encampment as if for prayer, cross the plain, and ascend the hill to Bethulia, where they display Holofernes' head. The body is left to be discovered the next morning as the Hebrew army descends on the now-leaderless Assyrians, whom the Hebrews slaughter as they flee. In the biblical narrative, the Jewish warriors are named "filii Israhel" (sons of Israel, 15:3). In the poem, however, they are repeatedly called "Ebreas" (Hebrews, 241, 298, 305). Along with Judith's trinitarian prayer, the use of "Hebrews" for the Jewish people makes clear the poem's Christological understanding of the Hebrew Bible only as a prelude to Christianity.[26]

Pagans, Jews, and Christians in Early Christianity

The lives of Margaret of Antioch and Helen (Elene), the mother of Constantine, take place in the first centuries of the Common Era, after the birth and death of Jesus and the advent of Christianity. Rather than opposing Hebrews to heathens, they set Christians against pagans in the *Life of St. Margaret* and against Jews in *Elene*. Margaret was a very popular saint in the Middle Ages, and her legend survives in several versions in England, in both Old English and Latin. Two Old

---

[26] Hill, 1981, demonstrates that the prayers in *Daniel* and *Judith* follow the tradition of Irish *lorica* (breastplate) prayers, which invoke the Trinity specifically for protection in time of great peril. In this reading too the Jewish characters are seen as proto-Christians.

English *Lives* in British Library MS Cotton Tiberius A.iii (eleventh century; hereafter Tiberius) and in Cambridge, Corpus Christi College 196 (twelfth century; Corpus) vary in significant details (Clayton and Magennis 1994).

St. Margaret's *Life* frequently uses animals in religious metaphors. The fifteen-year-old Margaret is tending sheep, evoking the Christian metaphor of priests as shepherds and congregations as their flocks, when a prefect, Olibrius, catches sight of her and immediately desires her. His soldiers seize Margaret. The metaphor then shifts, highlighting Margaret's sheeplike vulnerability: Margaret prays, saying she is "swa swa nytenu onmiddan felde and swa swa spærwe on nette and swa swa fisc on hoce" (like cattle in a field, like a sparrow in a net, and like a fish on a hook, Tiberius §5). The Corpus text also has wolves attacking Margaret-as-sheep. Margaret's opponents, however, are also linked with animals. In Tiberius, Margaret calls the prefect "ungeþunggena hund" (base dog, §10); in Corpus, she prays for help "for me beoð abuton hundes swa manega" (because there are so many dogs around me, §10). The detail recalls the moment when Holofernes, still clinging to life, is called "hæðenan hund" (heathen dog, *Judith* 110). Ecofeminist philosophers focus on gender as a marker of human divisions but acknowledge that there are others; men with outsider status, whether marked by ethnicity, religion, class, or geographic origin, were regularly depicted as animallike. Non-Christian antagonists are demeaned by animal metaphors in these texts.

Margaret is visited by a devil in the form of a dragon with menacingly shining eyes named Rufus (Latin: Red, §12), who breathes smoke and fire. A second devil appears, "sweart and unfæger, swa swa him gecynde wæs" (black and ugly, just like his character, Corpus §14), and Margaret conquers him with physical force. She prays and a cross appears from heaven, carried by an angel (Corpus) or accompanied by a dove (Tiberius). When on the following day Olibrius places Margaret into a cauldron of boiling water, emissaries return; "ure Drihten him self com of heofonum to eorþan astigan" (our Lord himself came down from heaven to earth, Corpus §20). Angels sing, and people who are ill or impaired touch Margaret's body and are healed. In an intriguing reversal of *Judith*, in which the heroine brings Holofernes' head up the mountain to the fortified city of Bethulia, leaving his body to be found by his troops in the morning, some versions of the Margaret legend depict angels carrying Margaret's head to heaven, leaving her body on Earth as a healing relic.

Olibrius' religious affiliation is somewhat contradictory in the various versions. Roman prefects would have been pagan until after the conversion of Constantine in 313, narrated in the Old English *Elene* discussed next. Christians were persecuted, as Jews had been, because they refused to worship Roman gods. The Tiberius text first refers to God "þe wæs ahangen fram Iudeum" (who was hanged by Jews).[27] Then, Olibrius asks Margaret if she believes in "þone Crist þe min fæderas ahengon" (that Christ whom my ancestors hanged, §6); she replies, "Þine fæderas Crist ahengon and þy hi ealle forwurdon" (Your ancestors hanged Christ and for that they all perished, §6). Later, Olibrius demands that Margaret "gebid þe to minum gode" (pray to my god, §17) – referring to God as singular, again suggesting that he is a Jewish prefect. The Corpus text never mentions the Jews, and Margaret refers at several other points to the "gods" of Olibrius, suggesting that she blames Romans, rather than Jews, for Jesus' death, though this would be unusual for early medieval England. In different ways, the two Old English versions heighten the iniquity of Olibrius and the bystanders, in Corpus by associating pagan gods with witchcraft, and in Tiberius by conflating Romans and Jews, whom many other texts distinguished, probably because Christian authors and audiences saw them as aligned in error.

Pagans, Christians, and Jews coexisted, often uneasily, in the early centuries of the Common Era. Roman officials punished Jews and Christians alike for refusing to worship their gods, but Old English writers largely ignore the persecution of Jews, though emphasizing the difficulties faced by early Christians.[28] After the conversion of Emperor Constantine in 313 CE, and the adoption of Christianity as the official state religion as narrated in *Elene*, the positions of Christians, pagans, and Jews shifted, with pagans who might not have had the opportunity to hear the Gospels considered potential converts, but Jews derided as either wicked, because they rejected Christian interpretation of Hebrew scripture, or blind, because they did not understand the "Old Testament" as Christians did or believe that Jesus was God's son.

The Christianization of the Roman Empire

Bede's official narrative described a thorough and fairly quick English conversion from paganism to Christianity, but the reality was much more complex; some kings adopted Christianity while others followed pagan rites. The evidence of place-names, especially farther away from churches and village centers, suggests that pagan beliefs existed alongside Christian ones for centuries. Politically, the Jews became useful figures of disapprobation to unite

---

[27] Note, however, that as the Gospels themselves attest, the Roman governor crucified Jesus; crucifixion was a Roman, not a Jewish, practice.

[28] In a rare early medieval English treatment of Roman persecution of Jews, Ælfric retells parts of the book of Maccabees, praising Jews who resisted or were martyred rather than compromise their faith. Yet he contrasts these pious Jews with contemporary Jews "þe urne drihten forseoð" (who despise our Lord, Clayton and Mullins 2019, vol. 2, *The Martyrdom of the Maccabees*, 69). He denounces Jews again at 72–3 and 521–72 and predicts their final conversion to Christianity, after the deaths of many, 528–30.

a sometimes pagan-leaning English laity. The Old English poetic adaptation of the Latin *Inventio Sanctae Crucis* (*Finding of the Holy Cross*), known as *Elene*, proved a powerful vehicle for that project, contrasting the pagan Constantine's ready acceptance of Christianity with a depiction of the Jews as mendacious, obstinate, and antagonistic to Christian doctrine.

Elene opens with Rome under attack from a vast army of "Huna leode ond Hreðgotan / . . . Francan ond Hugas" (Hunnish people and Hrethgoths . . . Franks and Hugas, Krapp, 1932, 20, 21b). Constantine, seeing the massed enemy troops, is "afyrhted, / egsan geaclad" (afraid, frightened with horror, 56b–57a). The night before battle, he is startled awake by a messenger who tells him to look to the sky to see a "sigores tacen" (symbol of victory, 85a), gleaming with gold and jewels, inscribed with the message, "Mid þys beacne ðu / . . . feond oferswiðesð" (With this beacon . . . you will vanquish your enemy, 92b, 93b).

Constantine orders a replica of the cross from his vision to be fashioned and carried before the army as a battle standard; he wins. Afterward, he asks his advisors what this sign means, and the text briefly summarizes Jesus' life and attributes his death to the Jews, saying that "se ealda feond" (the ancient enemy, i.e., Satan, 207b) seduced "Iudea cyn, þæt hie god sylfne / ahengon" (Jewish people, so that they hanged God himself, 209–210a). The Jews are depicted as a single unified body, here and later in the poem, while Christians are individualized.

Constantine orders his mother, Helen (Elene), to sail with an army to Jerusalem to find the buried original cross. There, she harangues groups of Jewish men, calling them blind, sinful, foolish, and damned, and telling them about biblical passages Christians take to prophesy Jesus, as spoken by Moses, David, Solomon, and Isaiah. The Jews tell her "anmode" (with one mind, 396) that they do not understand what sin they have committed. Each group of Jews is treated as a large number of interchangeable entities, any possible differences among them flattened by their disagreement with Christian doctrine. Eventually Judas tells the other Jews that he knows what Helen wants: the "sigebeam" (victory-cross, 420) on which Jesus was tortured and whom "þurh hete hengon on heanne beam / in fyrndagum fæderas usse" (our ancestors hanged through hate on a high beam in days of old (425–6). Judas tells the other Jews that his grandfather and father passed on the story of Jesus' death and resurrection, each telling the next generation to reveal the information when asked. While in other texts, pagans or Christians blame Jews for the death of Jesus, *Elene* gives the idea to the Jews themselves, rendering it confession rather than accusation.

The Jews do not give Helen this new information. The narrative therefore represents them as sinful and mendacious, as Helen has accused them of being. Finally, as a group they give up Judas and tell Helen that he knows what she wants. Judas too is depicted as obdurate, telling her he knows nothing of the cross or the place it was buried. Earlier in the text, Helen had accused the Jews of blaspheming the writings that they had learned from their forefathers (387b–388a). The scene in which Judas refuses to give her the information he has received from his father makes her accusation narratively real.

Judas relents only after Helen has confined him in a dry well without food for seven days and nights. He adds that he now recognizes "ðæt soð" (the truth, 708a) and will tell her where to find the cross. Judas' delayed and opportunistic acceptance of Christianity, motivated primarily by hunger, is contrasted with Constantine's instantaneous conversion. The circumstances are quite different: Constantine is promised victory in war if he will accept and display the cross, while Judas has been warned of the dissolution of his community if he reveals what he knows. The poet depicts Judas as knowing the truth all along but deliberately choosing sin and heresy. At length, he is converted, and the poem characterizes Judaism as "deofulgildum, ond gedwolan fylde, / unrihte æ" (idolatry, the pursuit of heresy, and sinful custom, 1040–1041a). After Judas has been baptized as Cyriacus, Helen asks him to find the nails used to fasten Jesus to the cross. When he does so, a miraculous ray of light shines forth from them and the people of Jerusalem accept Christianity, once again "ealle anmode" (all of one mind, 1117a). Thus the poem enacts the fantasy that all Jews will convert to Christianity when shown a miracle. The poem ends with no Jews left in Jerusalem – a false situation that affects early English depictions of contemporary Jerusalem. For monks and priests in early medieval England who were confronting lingering pagan practices and beliefs, mass conversion must have been a welcome fantasy.

Christians and Jews in the Early Middle Ages

Alongside such imagined textual accounts of Jerusalem and its environs, documentary sources from the early medieval period depict contemporary holy lands. Adomnán, Irish monk and abbot of the monastery at Iona (on the west coast of Scotland), wrote *De locis sanctis* (*On the Holy Lands*) in the 680s based on travels by Bishop Arculf of Gaul and older sources, especially the early Christian writers Hegesippus, Jerome, and Sulpicius Severus. Bede abridged Adomnán's work, adding and modifying it based on other texts (Fraipont, 1965); he quotes highlights from this abridgement in his *Ecclesiastical History* (V.15–17). Both of his versions were widely read (Colgrave and Mynors, 1969, lxxv–vi), but the translator of the Old English *Bede* omitted this section.

Descriptions of pilgrimage helped English readers imagine themselves on journeys they could not personally make. Audiences learn the names of the six gates to Jerusalem, for instance (Meehan, 1958, I.1.3). Arculf visits a market with "diuersarum gentium undique prope innumera multitudo" (diverse peoples from everywhere, an almost uncountable multitude, I.1.8). Detailed descriptions and measurements are given for the marvelously constructed Church of the Holy Sepulchre (I.2.1–15), quite different from small wood or wattle-and-daub English buildings. Adomnán tells of many more churches and sites of biblical stories, such as where Abraham built an altar to sacrifice his son Isaac (I.6.2). Jerusalem marks the center of the Earth: at midday on the solstice, the sun shines directly down and casts no shadow (I.11.2–3; it is not quite true, but the shadow is less than at higher latitudes).

In Hygeburg's *Hodoeporicon*, Willibald and his companions visit locations of importance in the Christian Bible. The tomb of St. John is "in loco specioso" (in a beautiful place, Holder-Egger, 1887, 93.17; cf. Talbot, 1954, 160). After seeing John's tomb, the monks go to a larger city, beg for bread, and sit on the edge of a fountain to eat – an idyllic moment a modern tourist can appreciate, rather than an experience sought out based on a guidebook. In a more frightening episode, Willibald goes blind for two months, but his sight is restored at a church situated where the cross of Jesus' crucifixion was found (99.12–16; Talbot, 1954, 168). Willibald had been to other holy sites between the onset of his blindness and his cure, yet readers might be struck that his sight returns at the same place the cross was first seen again after centuries, the story recounted in *Elene*. Textual and personal experience are woven tightly together.

Pilgrimage seems to have been normal, though not common, for Western European people in the early Middle Ages: an adventure that few make in person and that more follow via written accounts. Arculf meets a Burgundian named Peter and joins him for a time on his journeys (Meehan, 1958, II.26.5). Willibald leaves Rome with two companions (Holder-Egger, 1887, 92.27; Talbot, 1954, 159), but by the time of his arrival at Emesa, he has eight (94.13; Talbot, 1954, 162). At Emesa, an interpreter tells officials that he has often seen these men's countrymen and that they come from the west, where the sun sets (94.19–20 and 95.11–12; Talbot, 1954, 162–3). Apparently, pilgrims are rare enough that Emesan officials do not have a regular protocol for handling them, yet the old man has seen pilgrims from Britain before. Pilgrimages continue through the time of the Norman Conquest. Swein, son of Earl Godwine, arrived in Jerusalem successfully but died attempting to return in 1052, and Bishop Ealdred of Worcester traveled two years later (Pelteret, 2014, 88–91; see also 80–2 for Wythman and 92–4 for Ingulf).

Accounts from pilgrims scarcely acknowledge the existence of contemporary Jews in and around Jerusalem but make Christianity central. Adomnán uses the negative term "Iudaei" for Jews from Christ's lifetime and later. One anecdote describes the "credulus Iudaeus" (believing Jew, I.9.2) who takes a burial cloth from Jesus' tomb for safekeeping. Yet he is also called a "felix et fidelis furax" (blessed and faithful thief, I.9.3) who keeps the cloth to himself, alliteration tying the positives to the negative to create paradox. The thief's heirs squabble over the cloth because it brings increased wealth to the holder; in this story, both see value in Jesus' burial cloth yet do not have (full) faith in him. Eventually, Christians regain it (I.9.15). These Jews appear well in the past, not as people contemporary pilgrims could meet, even in Jerusalem.

Like *De locis sanctis*, *The Hodoeporicon* hardly mentions Jews except to refer to many churches and "synagogues of the Jews" in Tiberius, then a center of Jewish life (95.33; Talbot, 1954, 164). Hygeburg also tells a story of Jews trying to seize the body of Mary, the mother of Jesus, before angels came to take her to heaven (97.4–98.7; Talbot, 1954, 166). Here, Jews appear both malicious and ignorant – and well in the past. Their arms become stuck to the bier carrying Mary's body until the apostles pray and God releases them. Jews then vanish from the text again; readers could imagine that no Jewish people still lived in and around Jerusalem, in keeping with *Elene*'s depiction of Jewish mass conversion. This seems particularly odd in contrast with the reference to the "the country of the Samaritans" (100.20; cf. Talbot, 1954, 169) as a contemporary identifier. For more positive references to Jewish people of the past, both Adomnán and Hygeburg use the term "children of Israel" (Holder-Egger, 1887, 97.2; Talbot, 1954, 165; Meehan, 1958, II.14.1): different names separate these virtuous believers from the time before Jesus from often-vilified contemporary Jews and lay the groundwork for outright racial hatred later.

Muslims in the Early Middle Ages

By the time of these pilgrimages, Muslims ruled a wide area, including Jerusalem and other sites that they, as well as Jews and Christians, held sacred. Both Adomnán's text and Hygeburg's show some interest in geopolitics: Arculf identifies Damascus as the seat of the caliphate (II.28.1), and *The Hodoeporicon* explains that Emesa is in Syria and under Muslim control. Both invariably call Muslims "Saracens," after common but false patristic and medieval claims that Muslims named themselves for Sarah, Abraham's wife, to pretend they descended from her and hide the supposed shame of their actual lineage from Hagar, Abraham's servant. The name itself implies they cannot be trusted (Scarfe Beckett, 2003, 93–7). Shokoofeh Rajabzadeh (2019) compellingly argues that to repeat the term "Saracen" without critique reenacts the racist violence of this false etymology. The term predates Islam and does not always name Muslims, but the texts discussed here use it for Muslims.

Adomnán criticizes Muslims in Jerusalem because where the magnificent Temple once stood, on its ruins now stands what he characterizes as a crudely constructed, wooden Muslim house of prayer (I.1.14). Yet this building can hold 3,000, and surely the size would seem impressive to early English readers. Adomnán labels the Muslims of Damascus "Saracinorum ... incredulorum" (unbelieving Saracens, II.28.2). No early medieval English text attests any attempt to understand Islam. Neither Bishop Arculf nor any of the monks seek to convert anyone, though contemporary English missionaries traveled to Northern and Central Europe in search of potential pagan converts (see Section 2). Nor do any Muslims attempt to convert Christians. A Muslim king, Mavias, treats a burial cloth from Jesus' tomb "cum magna reuerentia" (with great reverence, I.9.11) and relies on God to decide its fate (and God promptly gives it to Christians, I.9.15).[29] Yet he remains Muslim, and no one suggests he should adopt Christianity.

In the *Hodoeporicon*, when Willibald and his fellow travelers can provide no credentials, Syrian officials arrest them (Holder-Egger, 1887, 94.13–17; Talbot, 1954, 162). Yet while the monks are imprisoned, officials allow meals, baths, and visits to a church and a market every Sunday; a Spaniard uses family connections at the caliphate court to free them (94.13–95.17; Talbot, 1954, 162–3). When the companions later seek the caliph for a letter of safe conduct, they cannot meet him because of disease in the area, not for religious or political reasons (100.4–8; Talbot, 1954, 169). Christians live alongside Muslims and go to their own church. Hygeburg's most negative portrayal of Muslims comes in reference to a church in Nazareth: "The Christians have often had to come to terms with the pagan Saracens about this church, because they wished to destroy it" (95.23–4; Talbot, 1954, 163). "Pagan" was always a derogatory term, from *paganus*, "of the country, of a village, rustic": the word labels people crude and ignorant simply for not being Christian (Lewis and Short, 1879; and Latham, Howlett, and Ashdowne, 1975–2013). This pairing of "Saracen" and "pagan" marks these Muslims at the moment of the most charged encounter between the two religions in the text. Yet the Muslims have not destroyed the church; they have only been described as wanting to do so. The text juxtaposes negative depictions of Muslims as dishonest and antagonistic with portrayals of them coexisting peacefully with Christians.

None of these texts give physical descriptions of Muslims; they are not set apart by any visual attribute, only by religion. At one point, a man traveling with the monks, apparently as a guide, is called "an Ethiopian" (100.22; Talbot,

---

[29] For the identity of Mavias as Muʿāwiya I (d. 680), founder of the Umayyad caliphate, see Scarfe Beckett, 2003, 45.

1954, 170); as Scarfe Beckett notes, this designation might refer to darker skin (2003, 50). English writers show no interest in Muslim beliefs, only emphasizing that they are wrong because they do not worship the Christian Trinity. David Pelteret argues for a shift after the Norman Conquest from "religion … as a private spiritual quest" to religion "as a belief system that should be imposed on others" (2014, 78). English participation in the First Crusade (1096–9) was limited, but it would grow in later Crusades.

Bede shows more hostility to Muslims, particularly those outside Palestine, in his original works than he does in his adaptations and translations (Scarfe Beckett, 2003, 122–39). In his commentary on the book of Genesis, Bede describes Muslims overwhelming all of Africa, most of Asia, and part of Europe (quoted in Scarfe Beckett, 2003, 129). In the universal chronicle in his *De temporum ratione* (*On the Reckoning of Time*), Bede writes of Sicily that Muslims "invadunt" and "praeda nimia … ablata" (invaded and carried off excessive plunder, Jones 1977, chapter 66, lines 1880–1) . Muslims also destroyed Carthage at the end of the seventh century (66, 1930–3) and for three years besieged Constantinople, whose people prayed until famine, cold, and pestilence killed so many Muslims that they retreated. They suffered more losses in a rout by the Bulgars (66, 2052–60), but, having learned nothing from their defeats, they depopulated Sardinia and dug up the bones of St. Augustine of Hippo, which King Liutprand of the Lombards ransomed back (66, 2061–6). Bede ends his world chronicle here and then treats the end times, linking Muslims to apocalypse. Muslims appear only once in his *Ecclesiastical History*, as a plague (*lues*, V.23) devastating Gaul who receive an unspecified but fitting punishment. Unlike Christians, Muslims have no names or individuality in any of these works, and Bede presents them as enemies of God and Christians.

Conclusion

To early medieval English people, historical and contemporary realities overlay each other in Jerusalem and its environs. Even as some people had more immediate knowledge of the region through trade, diplomatic relations, and pilgrimage, their relationships with these distant places were also informed by written sources. Texts set securely in the past portrayed sites of heroism and faith by a few exceptional Jews and later by Christians. The existence of contemporary Jews and Muslims who did not share Christian faith troubled ongoing English connections through trade and pilgrimage. A desire for connection with and knowledge of Jerusalem as the "Holy Land" coexisted with misunderstanding and hostility toward the Jews and Muslims who lived there.

4 Asia and Africa

Early medieval English writers described the non-European world in ways that foregrounded difference. Imagining bodies as larger, hairier, and darker skinned than those of Europeans, combining human and animal parts, or transcending gender expectations allowed them to imagine themselves – male, Christian, English – as "normal," their physical characteristics in need of no explanation. Authors showed significant interest in both Asia and Africa, sometimes treating them as they would places closer to home, but sometimes describing them as exotic or frightening. As Mary Kate Hurley puts it: "Monsters and marvels are dangerous because they highlight difference, they confuse observers, and they hijack language for their own monstrous purposes" (2016, 843). Histories, saints' lives, homilies, and wonder texts reveal how the English saw Asia and Africa. The Old English *Orosius* preserves Paulus Orosius' original view of North Africa as simply part of a wider Roman world, with Carthage as a center of power often competing with Rome. The Old English translation of the *Soliloquies* identifies the church father Augustine, more commonly identified with Hippo, as the bishop of Carthage; the *Martyrology* also identifies him as African. More sustained depictions of the non-European world, as known and imagined, are found in texts collected in two manuscripts that overlap in surprising ways. This section focuses on aspects of those texts containing descriptions of actual geographical, zoological, and ethnic or cultural groups, while Section 5 deals with "imagined lands," including further depictions of Asia and Africa. The early medieval English were fascinated by these continents and both connected with and defined themselves against them.

Divisions of the World

Early medieval European Christians generally thought in terms of three continents, each with its own peoples. The biblical book of Genesis tells of a great flood that destroyed all life on Earth except Noah, his wife, his sons, his sons' wives, and the animals in his ark. In Genesis 9:20–7, Noah becomes drunk. Ham sees him naked and tells his brothers, who cover Noah without looking. When Noah wakes, he blesses Japheth and curses Ham and his descendants to serve his brothers.[30] Ælfric transmits the idea that each continent is given to one of Noah's sons: "Asia on eastrice þam yldstan suna, Affrica on suðdæle þæs Chames cynne, 7 Europa on norðdæle Iapheþes ofspringe" (Asia in the eastern kingdom to the oldest son, Africa in the southern part to the kin of Cham, and Europe in the northern region to the

---

[30] Genealogies connected with the West Saxon court introduced a fourth son, Sceaf, born to Noah on the ark, from whom the English are descended. For more about the three or four sons and their descendants, see Anlezark, 2002.

descendants of Japheth, Crawford, 1922, 280–3). Privileging the ancestor of Europeans and diminishing the forebear of Africans had far-reaching effects on ideas of the lands and peoples. The Cotton World Map (see Section 1) depicts political regions and cities among mountains, rivers, and seas in Asia and Africa. Asia takes up roughly the top half of the map, which is oriented to the east; the bottom half is divided between Europe and Africa, with Europe somewhat larger. In addition to actual places and peoples, the Cotton World Map includes gryphons and cynocephali in Africa and Asia respectively, thus combining the real with the fabulous as wonder texts do.

Africa and Asia are nebulously defined in many Old English texts. Ælfric writes of "þone east dæl middan eardes þe is gehate asia" (the east part of middle earth, that is called Asia, MacLean, 1884, 370–1) and also comments that the world was divided into "ðri dælas" (three regions, Crawford, 1922, 279). In *Saint Eugenia*, however, Ælfric writes that Eugenia's two brothers were appointed to positions of honor, "ænne on Affrican and oðerne on Cartagine" (one in Africa and one in Carthage, Clayton and Mullins 2019, vol. 1, 322), suggesting that he understands each as a separate city or region, rather than Africa as a continent encompassing Carthage. The Old English *Orosius* divides the oceans and the land masses into three parts, "þeah þe sume men sæden þæt þær nære buton twegen dælas: Asia 7 þæt oþer Europe" (though some men said that there are only two regions: Asia, and the other Europe, Bately, 1980, 8.14–15). The text describes continental boundaries by landmarks including the Don and Nile Rivers and the city of Alexandria; the translator shows some independence of the Latin here – and more confidence than most Old English writers seem to have about the continents, despite inaccuracies such as Daniel Anlezark describes in the geography of India (2022).

Trade

The English had both direct and indirect trade with parts of Asia and Africa. A coin of Offa of Mercia closely resembles a 773–4 dinar of ʿAbbāsid caliph al-Manṣūr. Rory Naismith argues that the mint must have had an original dinar as a model but notes that "Offa Rex" is inverted from the Arabic description; the moneyer could not recognize the writing's orientation, let alone read it (2005, 197). The coin symbolically puts Offa on a level with ʿAbbāsid rulers, showing they held prestige for eighth-century Mercians. Finds of whole coins suggests that their value lay not only in the precious metal but also *as* coins from a powerful authority.[31] We do not know how the prototype dinar or any of the 173 extant Islamic coins from before

---

[31] Thirty-eight coins in Naismith's appendices (2005) are whole; more than thirty are fragments and may have been used as hack silver, valued for weight rather than as a coin. Many have unrecorded or uncertain conditions.

1100 reached England. Yet the number of coins, range of dates, and evidence that early medieval England may have had far more Islamic coins than are now extant suggest multiple contacts, some direct.[32]

English references to incense, spices, lapis lazuli, and silks show networks of exchange with West Asia. Cuthbert's letter on the death of Bede notes that Bede had pepper and incense to give as gifts (Colgrave and Mynors, 1969, 585). Elias, the patriarch of Jerusalem, sent letters and gifts to Alfred, and *Bald's Leechbook* contains a section of medical recipes from Elias, some apparently directed for Alfred's specific health problems.[33] These and other Old English recipes contain more than eighty mentions of pepper, suggesting wide availability (Healey, 2009). Ælfric's *Saint Edmund* describes the thin line where the saint's decapitated head miraculously reconnected to his dead body as a silk thread (179): he expects audiences to know how silk looks (Clayton and Mullins, 2019, vol. 2, lines 167–8). *Bald's Leechbook* recommends silk thread for sutures. The ships used by pilgrims such as Arculf and Willibald were trading ships willing to take on passengers (Scarfe Beckett, 2003, 47). Daniel Anlezark (2022) argues that the pilgrims Alfred sent with alms to Rome and India, or possibly Judea, would also have been scouting trade routes.

Religion

Religion was a source of ongoing contact with the other continents. When the archbishop-elect of Canterbury died of plague in Rome around 667, the pope asked Abbot Hadrian, "vir natione Afir" (a man of African race, Bede, *HE* IV.1), to take his place. Hadrian initially refused, and eventually the pope appointed Theodore of Tarsus on the condition that Hadrian accompany him to Britain. Bede praises Hadrian for his knowledge of the Bible, church practices, Greek, and Latin. A whole school of English biblical commentary grew from the teachings of Hadrian and Theodore. Hadrian remained in England for forty years and imported music, liturgical changes, and cults of saints not previously celebrated in England, making a considerable impact on English learning and religion (Rambaran-Olm, 2021). The Old English *Bede* retains the reference to Hadrian's Italian monastery but omits the phrase identifying his origin, making him seem Italian rather than African. The translator thus erases the African origins of Hadrian's intellectual contributions to England.[34] Yet the Old English

---

[32] Naismith, 2005, notes that the Cuerdale Hoard had thirty-six to fifty Islamic coins originally, but now there are only twenty-nine.

[33] For Elias, see Asser, chapter 91 (Stevenson, 1959). For recipes, see Keynes and Lapidge, 1983, 270n220, and Anlezark, 2022.

[34] The translator generally downplays contributions from outside England, omitting some documentation from abroad and even mention of it, though he continues to emphasize England's ties

Exodus starts with the departure from the "Sigelwara land" (Ethiopians' land, Krapp, 1931, 69) and concludes with the rejoicing of an "Afrisc meowle" (African woman, 580) at the Israelites' escape and the destruction of the Egyptians.[35] Bioarchaeological researchers have found skeletons in four English communities dating from the seventh through eleventh centuries that have characteristics demonstrating Mediterranean or African origins. "These skeletons confirm that there were people of African descent in the communities that made up the various audiences of *Exodus* ... whose existence has been largely whitewashed out of modern scholarship and popular history" (Dockray-Miller, 2022, 466). Some Old English texts obscure religious ties with Africa, while others recognize them in ways supported by the archaeological record.

Numerous poetic and prose texts in Old English and Anglo-Latin describe the travels of apostles, saints, and bishops into lands beyond the reach of Christianity to convert the locals to their faith.[36] Most scholars of medieval England have taken this at face value, though some now recognize that traveling to places as a foreigner, calling devotees of other religions "heathens," and asking them to adopt one's religion and culture is, at best, problematic. But English intrusions are characterized as benevolent rather than culturally violent, and when a missionary is killed, the people are characterized as vicious, savage "barbarians." The poem *Fates of the Apostles*, inscribed in the Vercelli Book alongside *Andreas*, *Elene*, and several prose homilies, states that Phillip was killed "mid Asseum" (among the Asians, Krapp, 1932, 38) in "Gearapolim" (40) – that is, Hierapolis, in present-day Turkey. Simon and Thaddeus preach in Persia, while Thomas and Bartholomew go to India; the latter was beheaded "forþan he ða hæðengild hyran ne wolde, / wig weorðian" (because he did not wish to follow heathen worship or honor idols, 47–48a). Most *Chronicle* texts record that in 883 or 884, King Alfred sent emissaries with alms to Rome and to Saint Thomas, in India or Judea.

In Ælfric's *Saint Thomas*, Thomas goes to India and persuades many people to adopt Christianity, largely through miracles in which he raises the dead and heals "deafe and blinde" (deaf and blind [people], 187) and "healte and blinde" (lame and blind [people], Clayton and Mullins 2019, vol. 3, 246). Thomas uses these Indian people, identified only by their disability, to demonstrate that his religion is superior to theirs, and Ælfric further deploys them to demonstrate

---

with Rome. The omission of Hadrian's origins preserves ties to Italy while reducing influence from elsewhere. See Discenza, 2002.

[35] See Jill Fitzgerald, forthcoming, for this figure and how modern emendations have obscured her, changing race, gender, or both. Scholars who accept the manuscript reading sometimes argue for reading her as Miriam, Moses' sister, or Zipporah, Moses' Ethiopian wife. Fitzgerald emphasizes the character's role in reclaiming the community's story.

[36] See Section 3 for English interest in converting pagans but not Jews or Muslims.

Thomas' holiness. While not monstrous, they differ from Ælfric's (unstated) masculine norm, and they are identified only as abstract embodiments of illness and disability. One such woman is given the name Sintice (263), but besides the fact of her blindness, we learn nothing. Thomas is in India because the king's steward needed workmen to build a palace in what he considers the more advanced "romanisce" (Roman, 39) style of Thomas' home province, Caesarea. Thomas is brought before what Ælfric calls the "bysmorfullum anlicnyssum" (abominable images, 402) of the Indians' "lifleasum godum" (lifeless gods, 400), and destroys them; he is then killed.

The early medieval English presentation of non-Christian gods as abhorrent is thoroughgoing, extending to Judaism and Islam, as well as to the pagan gods of the English. English Christians saw themselves as direct descendants of Old Testament Jews, comparing their journey from Scandianavia and Northern Europe to the Jews' passage across the Red Sea (Howe, 1989). This parallel allows English Christians to honor pagan forebears such as Beaw and even Woden, reduced from a god to a human ancestor (see Section 1), while declaring paganism superseded, much as they also venerated some Jews in the Hebrew Bible as "pre-Christian worthies." But the presentation of local religion as abominable and the use of disabled people as props in saintly careers must be read in the context of the sustained discussions of Asia and Africa in wonder texts. The beliefs that non-Christian religions are contemptible and that the peoples of Asia and Africa must be induced to convert to Christianity would, unfortunately, provide an intellectual framework that informed missionaries, fortune hunters, and colonizers in later centuries.

Monsters and Wonders

Three wonder texts present people in Africa and Asia as unusual and even monstrous. *The Letter of Alexander to Aristotle* (see also Section 2), purportedly by Alexander the Great, includes animals, peoples, and even individuals that are historically attested, as well as marvelous and monstrous creatures; it circulated in Latin versions and was translated into Old English. *Wonders of the East* and the *Liber Monstrorum* are by and large catalogues of fables, and they mention names of actual places and peoples as well. The *Wonders* (or *Marvels*) *of the East* is an Old English translation of a Latin collection of marvels that names places in Asia, including Babylon, Persia, the Red Sea, and the Nile River. The *Liber Monstrorum* or *Book of Monsters* is a Latin compendium of lore drawn from Isidore, Augustine, and Orosius' *History*. Though the five surviving manuscripts were all written in mainland Europe, not in England, a reference to Hygelac as well as similarities to the prologue of the English writer

Aldhelm's *De Virginitate* have led scholars to propose an English origin; Christopher Monk argues that the *Liber* is an English production of the time if not the pen of Aldhelm (Monk, 2013, 93n47).

Wonders and the *Liber* are filled with imagined beings: human-animal hybrids and other monsters and marvels. Within *Wonders*, Old English "east" is used to render the Latin "orient" on three occasions, but always to refer to relative direction, not to characterize Asia or the non-European world as a whole. The people of early medieval England used the term "east" to refer to places and peoples that were far away and different from the English, a usage reflected in the title given in 1881.[37] For Ælfric and the author of the Old English *Orosius*, "the east" was generally Asia. *Wonders*, however, includes creatures identified with places in Africa on both the Cotton World Map and in the *Liber Monstrorum*. Designating *Wonders* as from "the east" in the modern title inaccurately represents how early English writers would have understood "east" geographically, but it accurately represents early English notions that Asia and Africa were places occupied by potentially dangerous others.

Wonders includes in its catalog of imagined places a few known lands and geographical features: Persia, Babylon, Media, India, Ethiopia, the Red Sea, and the Nile River, southeast of the British Isles rather than strictly east. The *Liber Monstrorum* likewise references real places, people, and geographical features in Europe as well as in Africa and Asia, including the Rhine and Nile Rivers; Italy, Sicily, and Mount Etna; the Mediterranean and Red Seas and the Indian Ocean; Europe, India, and "Oriente" (the East, Orchard, 1995, 26). These real places are juxtaposed with the underworld and the real people with monsters and animal-human hybrids, to depict a place outside of Europe, beyond the world that was well known, where even actual people take on the air of fable or monster. In representing differences in gender, physical appearance, and landscape, these depictions create a problematic context for works more focused on historical people and actual places, including the Alexander *Letter* and various saints' lives that figure Africa and Asia and the people in them in terms of alterity.

Asa Simon Mittman and Susan Kim point out that the *Liber Monstrorum* uses as an organizing principle the body of a female monster, linking femininity with the monstrosities depicted throughout the text (25), in an analogue to the depiction of female monsters at points where the text is ambiguous about

---

[37] The various versions of the text, as is standard practice in medieval manuscripts, contain no titles. Ann Knock's (1981) thorough review traces the term "orient" to a nineteenth-century editor who influenced Stanley Rypins, who titled the work "The Wonders of the East" in his influential edition for the Early English Text Society. Given the European ambitions of colonizing India and China in the nineteenth and early twentieth centuries, using "the East" in the title for a book of monsters and fables in locations to the south and southeast of England is surely ideologically interested.

gender. The first monster described in the *Liber* is a person "utriusque sexus" (of both sexes, I.1, 258) who appears to be a man but traps men "meretricis more" (in the fashion of a [female] prostitute, I.1). The *Liber* also describes as "incredibilibus" (incredible) another "genus untriusque sexus" (race of both sexes, I.19). Monstrosity, then, is in the first instance exemplified by ambiguity in gender, whether intersex, nonbinary, or trans. In modern medicine, intersex babies and children are often treated with surgery and/or hormones to bolster the fiction that gender comprises binary poles rather than a continuum. M. W. Bychowski provides examples of transgender individuals in the Middle Ages (2018), and with Dorothy Kim, points out that neither the word "medieval" nor the word "transgender" existed in the Middle Ages, "yet medieval and transgender describe realities that may exist regardless of whether a person whom they describe possessed the terminology" (Kim and Bychowski, 2019, 20). Trans and intersex people are dehumanized by their depiction in the *Liber* as monstrous.

Other physical features set Asian and African people apart from the English. The *Liber Monstrorum* describes Ethiopians as "toto corpore nigre" (dark in the entire body) because of exposure to "sol flagrans" (the blazing sun, I.9); another people is described as black "sicut Aethipoes" (like Ethiopians, I.30). In *Wonders*, pepper is black because it can be harvested only after lighting fires to frighten off the serpents that guard it (Fulk, 2010, 19), and there are people whose black skin is explained by their proximity to a flaming mountain or, like the Ethiopians, to the sun. There is no effort to explain the lighter skin color of Europeans, or of two groups of very tall people among the "wonders" with very fair skin (I.20, I.43). A similar note on skin color appears in the biblical poem *Exodus*, where Ethiopia contains "forbærned burh-hleoðu, brune leode, / hatum heofon-colum" (mountains and brown people, burned by the heat of the heaven's coal, 70–1). People, plants, and landscape bear the same effects of fire or the sun.

The *Liber* also describes various groups of cannibals, some dark skinned. Near the Red Sea, a people "commixtae naturae" (mixed in nature, I.40) speak many different languages so that they can trap people who have come from far away. They kill and eat them *crudos* (raw, I. 40), like a group of black-skinned giants living east of the River Brixontes who also eat people *crudos* (I.33). The range of meanings of *crudus* includes "cruel," "savage," and "merciless" as well as "raw" or "bleeding." Geraldine Heng locates the beginning of racialized skin color to the second half of the thirteenth century in medieval Europe, when a shift occurred in visual arts in depictions of Caucasians from pink or beige skin tones to white. "Whiteness was also eventually equated with colorlessness: 'By then it had become the norm for glass-painters to use colorless glass instead of flesh tints'" (2018, 183, quoting Madeline Caviness). As noted in Section 3, one of the devils who taunts St. Margaret in tenth-century *Lives* appears in the form of a black man, suggesting that blackness was already associated with and seen as a sign of sin and evil. Myths of black cannibals, giant or not, that were transmitted in early medieval England continued to circulate through the time of European travel to Africa and North America, thus conditioning what those later travelers would believe about the people they encountered.

The representation of the Earth as feminine bears comment. Old English is a language with grammatical gender, so that all words must be masculine, feminine, or neuter, with adjectives and other descriptive words modified to agree in form. Earth is seen as female beyond the accident of grammatical gender, however. Ecofeminist philosopher Val Plumwood traces the ways cultures from the Greeks forward have characterized the Earth as feminine; while Plumwood says very little about the Middle Ages, Rod Giblett comments specifically on Grendel's mother in his discussion of swamps as ambiguous, liminal, feminized landscapes (92–3). The Adam-Riddle characterizes the Earth as a womb from which Adam is born through God's intervention (Estes, 2012). Exeter Book Riddle 35 complicates things in that the object, usually solved as "ore," begins, "Mec se wæta wong, wundrum freorig, / of his innaþe ærist cende" (the wondrously cold and wet earth birthed me at first from his womb/belly, Krapp and Dobbie, 1936, 1–2). "Cennan" can mean to beget, usually considered the role of the father, and "innaþe" may refer to the stomach, intestines, or heart as well as to the womb. Like the intersex humans the *Liber* describes, it seems that the Earth fulfills the role of both father and mother in producing ore as "offspring."

The Letter of Alexander to Aristotle mostly names historical places, though some have fantastic traits. The Old English translation of the *Letter* begins with the statement that Alexander is writing to his former teacher "be þam þeod-londe Indie" (about the inhabited land of India, Fulk, 2010, 34), though it includes other places briefly. Like *Wonders* and the *Liber*, this text includes descriptions of real people, places, and animals juxtaposed with fantastic creatures: human-animal hybrids and people who differ from European norms in size or otherwise. The Cotton World Map contains an inscription near the edge of Asia labeling "India in qua sunt gentes xliiii" (India, in which there are forty-four peoples, Foys, Crossley, and Wacha, 2020); Alexander names many of them. He describes battles with Kings Darius of Persia and Porus of India, also recounted by the Old English *Orosius*. The lack of detail about Indians suggests that they are unremarkable, resembling Alexander's Greek soldiers. He wants to see the rest of the world, traveling by sea, but the locals tell him the sea is "to þon þiostre" (too dark) to be navigable by ship, so he goes instead to "þa wynstran dælas Indie" (the left-hand [i.e., northern] part of India, 64). He sees cynocephali (dog-headed men) in a place he describes as "oþer þeod-lond

India" (another region of India, 66), though these are located near the southern-most edge of Africa on the Cotton World Map.

The landscapes of the *Letter*, both built and natural, show a mix of familiar, fantastic, and threatening features. On entering Fasiacen, the royal city of King Porus, Alexander sees a hall with golden columns and golden walls. The inside walls are carved from ivory and decorated with various gems, with supporting columns made from cypress and laurel, trees not normally used as building materials in early medieval England. Alexander sees a vineyard with leaves of gold, and fruits of emerald, crystal, and other jewels (40). He adds, "Seldon we þær ænig seolfor fundon" (We rarely found any silver there, 40), as if silver is not precious enough. Descriptions of built structures that may be exaggerated but are plausible mix with imagined descriptions of fabulous plants. The landscape is fruitful in various ways, both "godra" (good) and "yfelra" (evil): "Hio is cennede þa ful-cuþan wildru ond wæstmas ond wecga oran ond wun-derlice wyhta" (she is the progenitor of the well-known wild animals and plants and lumps of ore, and wondrous creatures, 36).

The landscape itself is sometimes a hostile force: Alexander's journey is interrupted by boiling sands (weallende sond, 42), pestilential air (wol-berende lyft, 56), very strong wind (swiðe micel wind, 66), frost, snow, and raining fire (68). These may be meteorological phenomena: "boiling sands" could be caused by windstorm, or "raining fire" by a volcanic eruption. Somewhat improbably, Alexander and his troops traverse lands that are "monnum ungeferde for wildeorum ond wyrmum" (impenetrable to men because of wild animals and snakes, 64). They encounter a wide variety of known animals, including elephants (38, 46, and 64), horses and camels (46), hippopotami (50), lions, bears, tigers, leopards, and wolves (50), scorpions (52), rhinoceroses (56), crocodiles (64), and "hrifra wildeora" (violent wild animals, 40).

Notably, while "cynn" can refer to people, the Alexander *Letter* uses it only for objects, trees, and animals. He crosses terrain "missenlicra cynna eardung in wæs, nædrena ond rifra wildeora" (in which were diverse kinds of dwellings of serpents and abundant wild animals, 48). Later, in the sacred grove of the sun and the moon he learns: "Oþer þara is wæpned-cynnes sunnan trio, oþer wif-kynnes, þæt monan trio" (One of them is the male tree of the sun, the other the female tree of the moon, 70). Most astoundingly, the trees can speak and can foretell the future, and they tell Alexander that he will die the next May in Babylon (78).

One particularly revealing episode begins when Alexander attempts to slake his thirst in a river with undrinkably bitter water (46). Alexander and his men attempt to swim across the river; it is inhabited by water-monsters ("nicra," 50)[38] that attack the men, drag them to the river-bottom, and eat them. Alexander demands that some Indian men direct him to clean water; they send him to a large lake full of clear water. After his men make camp, "þa het ic ceorfan ða bearwas ond þone wudu fyllan þæt monnum wære þy eþre to þæm wæterscipe to ganganne" (then I ordered the groves cut down and the trees felled so that men could more easily go to the water, 52). From all the wood that they have just cut, Alexander orders that his men kindle 1,500 fires.

Killing the trees and scorching the Earth would destroy the local ecosystem and microclimate, likely making the water as undrinkable as that in the monster-filled river. From the viewpoint of Alexander and his soldiers, the river is infested with these hostile creatures. From a perspective foregrounding the natural environment and the non-human as well as human animals that populate it, however, Alexander and his men are strangers to the landscapes, animals, and human civilizations of India, looting, pillaging, and destroying built and natural environments without compunction. We might assume that an ecologically attuned perspective was foreign to the people of early medieval England, yet the Exeter Book Riddles are capable of imagining interactions between humans on the one hand, and animals, plants, and even ore on the other, from a non-human perspective, treating humans as aggressors in natural environments and calling the human the "feond" (enemy) of animals and plants (for example, Riddles 22, 26; Estes, 2017, chapter 5). In addition to felling trees, Alexander slaughters hundreds of animals and humans. Postcolonial ecocriticism helps to illuminate the presumption of European legitimacy and the connections among viewing land, animals, and kingdoms in comparable terms as open opportunities for pillage and plunder; from Alexander's viewpoint, and perhaps the Old English translator's, felling trees, killing animals, and slaughtering non-European people are morally equivalent, all justified to the great conqueror for his own purposes. Only Europeans are fully human in this view (Huggan and Tiffin, 2015; Deloughrey, 2014).

Alexander's massive destruction of the landscape echoes the clearing of land for agriculture from Neolithic times forward and prefigures modern deforestation. Similarly, Alexander denies agency to any beings he encounters in India—landscape, plants, animals, monsters, hybrids, and humans—treating them all as objects of his curiosity. He orders his human troops to kill other men; he also uses animals to destroy his Indian guides when they lead him to places of danger (Kim, 2010, 39). Everything in India is depicted as existing to serve Alexander's whims; plants, animals, humans, and monsters are undifferentiated in terms of Alexander's willingness to use them to his ends, or kill them when they do not

---

[38] Orchard (1995, 235) identifies these as hippopotami with reference to the Latin text.

meet his needs or desires. Some modern politicians encourage the destruction of wilderness areas and rainforests for the sake of global capitalism while denying climate change. Widespread contemporary views of animals and land as existing for humans, even in the framework of "stewardship" (Palmer, 2006), likewise deny agency to the non-human and, analogously, to various groups of humans.

Conclusion

Africa and Asia are often presented in early medieval England in both Latin and Old English as foreign places populated by humans and animals, monsters and marvels. Skin color is salient, and femininity in particular is aligned with monstrosity in *Wonders*, the *Liber*, and the Alexander *Letter*. In *Exodus*, Bede's *Ecclesiastical History*, and the Old English *Soliloquies* and *Orosius*, Africa appears as a place of military might and culture, while the wonder texts juxtapose "real" people of Asia and Africa with various "others," emphasizing a link between monstrosity and differences, which diverges from the writer's assumed but not explicitly stated norm in terms of gendered, ethnic, or tribal difference. All are subject to the European (male, Christian) gaze: in *Wonders* and the *Liber*, of the narrator; and in the *Letter of Alexander*, who was in the Middle Ages widely considered one of the "Nine Worthies" alongside King Arthur and Charlemagne. English treatment of Africa, Asia, and ultimately other continents as exotic, monstrous, and meant for use by Europeans would become more prominent in the centuries after the Norman Conquest.

5 Imagined Lands

Early medieval English representations of imagined lands include worlds out-side Europe and also closer to home. The deep seas, plumbed by Beowulf, traversed by the gannet and the swan, and inhabited by Grendel's mother and the whale, are both "here" and "elsewhere," but they cannot be visited by early medieval people and are depicted in fanciful terms. Wilderness in the lives of Guthlac is populated by demons and monsters, the terrain at once real and imagined as something apart. Old English poetic and prose texts locate mythical and monstrous beasts, as well as potentially frightening real animals, in "the East." Asia and Africa are actual places known to medieval Europeans through travel (see Section 4), but they were also imagined as home to a wide variety of fantastic and monstrous creatures in texts including the *Letter of Alexander*, the *Wonders of the East*, and the *Liber Monstrorum*. Mermedonia, where saints Matthew and Andrew converted the people to Christianity, is fully imagined. The dangers presented by these places and their inhabitants are offset by the mastery implied by descriptions, though fabulous, of witnesses who have visited them. The early English translators and writers of these tales define and therefore in a sense limit the unknown.

The Deep Sea

The deep sea can today be explored using submarine craft, but for early medieval English sailors and writers, it could only be imagined. The Exeter Book poem *The Whale* imagines a sly, malicious creature who floats at the surface until unwary seafarers, seeing what appears to be "hreofum stane" (rough stone, Krapp and Dobbie, 1936, 8b), anchor their ships, walk onto the apparent shore, and light fires. Once they have settled confidently, the whale "niþer gewiteþ / garsecges gæst, grund geseceð, / ond þonne in deaðsele drence bifæsteð / scipu mid scealcum" (enemy from the sea, departs downward, seeks bottom, and then in the death-hall commits ships with soldiers to drowning, 28b–31b). The whale, a malevolent creature of the deep sea that actively dupes and drowns seafarers, is like "deofla" (devils, 32) that lead people into evil, rather than an occupant of the sea with interests and goals different from those of the humans that travel across its surface in ships.

In *Beowulf*, the deep sea is likewise characterized as the realm of sea-monsters, in two different scenes. In boyhood, Beowulf and his friend Breca set out to swim the sea in a boast-driven contest; later, Beowulf swims down through the bottomless "mere" toward Grendel's mother in her lair. The animals and the waters they occupy are similarly characterized in terms of wild ferocity and hostility to human interlopers. Beowulf describes the bet that he and Breca can swim carrying "swurd nacod" (naked swords, Fulk, Bjork, and Niles, 2008, 539), with which "wit unc wið hronfixas werian þohton" (we two thought to protect ourselves against whales, 540–1). Beowulf and Breca swim for five days in "wado weallende" (tossing waves, 546), until they are driven apart by fierce winds in the cold night (546–8). Beowulf says he is attacked by a "fah feond-scaða" (a hostile enemy, 554), which drags him to the ocean bottom with "mod onhrered" (agitated mind, 549); he kills the attacker and eight other "niceras" (water-monsters, 575). He justifies killing these animals by saying that the sea-lanes are now safe for ships. The animals and the sea itself are exploited to demonstrate Beowulf's martial heroism and his ability to tell a tale.

Also close to home, yet impossibly far underground, Grendel's mother's "hof" (dwelling, 1507) is a subterranean cavern. Both England, where *Beowulf* was written, and Denmark, where it is set, have naturally occurring caves as well as caverns left by mining and quarrying. In the epic, such a cave becomes a home for monsters and the treasure they have collected. Beowulf swims for the better part of the day toward the underground lair. Numerous toothy fish attack, and eventually Grendel's mother grabs him and drags him inside in an echo of the Whale's actions: in both cases, humans can reach the sea floor only through the intervention of wild or monstrous creatures. Grendel and his mother are humanoid, though the whale and the wild beasts that Beowulf encounters on both of his journeys through the seas are fish-like. All have a common link with evil: the sea-beasts of *Beowulf* are merely hostile; the whale is diabolical; and the Grendelkin are descendants of Cain, the first murderer and progenitor of a race of monsters. The sea's surface enables human travels, even hosting joyous journeys, but its unknown depths are home to evil creatures figured as hostile to humans, their right to their own habitat never acknowledged.

European Wilderness

Because people cannot live in the sea, it is a kind of wilderness, untracked and untillable. Wilderness on land is also associated with monsters and devils. In *Beowulf*, Hrothgar tells the hero that Grendel and Grendel's mother have been seen wandering the boundary lands, far from human settlement. The area around their lair is characterized as both hellscape and wilderness. References to demons, flaming water, misty darkness, and cold cliffs recall descriptions of hell in the *Visio Pauli* and Blickling Homily 16 (Kelly, 2003, 144; see Section 6). The characterization of Grendel and his mother as demonic kinsmen of Cain heightens the hellishness of their underground lair, whose entrance is in a damp wilderness.

The poem's first reference to Grendel states that he "com of more under misthleoþum" (came from a moor with misty crags, 710). Old English "mor" is a wasteland, high, wet, or both (Bosworth, 1898). When Grendel flees after losing his arm to Beowulf, his lair is described as located "under fenhleoðu" (under fenbanks, 820), and after Grendel's mother has snatched the warrior Æschere to avenge his death, she is described as fleeing "to fenne" (to the fens, 1265). In Felix's *Vita*, Guthlac's fenland hermitage is a real place, but it is described in often fantastic terms as simultaneously trackless wilderness, the dwelling-place of various animals, location of ancient graves, and haunt of devils. The *Vita* describes the desolate fen where Guthlac seeks a hermitage as a region with wooded islands surrounded by marshes, bogs, and fog-shrouded black waters (Colgrave, 1956, 87). Guthlac engages a man named Tatwine to transport him by boat through "invia lustra" (trackless bogs, 89), which could also be rendered as "impassable wilderness," either translation contradicting Felix's statement that the area had previously been occupied and used as grave and then cistern, as well as Tatwine's knowledge of the region (Estes, 2017, 100).

The English fenlands were occupied during the early medieval period by nomadic people who fished the waters for eel but posed danger to anyone not intimately familiar with their twisting waterways and uncertain landscape (O'Brien O'Keeffe, 2001). In Guthlac's fenland, human and animal inhabitants are re-imagined as devils that torture the saint and speak in the sibilant language of the Britons. Guthlac had earlier been part of a Mercian invading force, fighting against inhabitants of the British Isles for military supremacy in a series of battles whose legitimacy has been challenged.[39] In claiming the fenland is unoccupied, Felix ignores both the animals and earlier human inhabitants. Deep-sea fish, whale, Grendelkin, and Britons are all cast as hostile and demonic in order to establish legitimacy for killing them. Neither *Beowulf* nor the *Life* of Guthlac sees a need to justify the treatment of animals, presented as irrelevant in the face of human interests, needs, or desires.

While the Grendelkin live in a naturally occurring underwater cave, the dragon has colonized a barrow, a grave mound full of ancient treasure. The dragon is usually identified as "wyrm" (worm, serpent, e.g., 2287), though occasionally the poem uses "draca" (dragon, e.g., 2290) from Latin *draco*. "Wyrm" is also used to refer to demons in hell (e.g., *Judith*, Dobbie, 1953, 115), associating the dragon congenitally with evil and sin, like the Grendelkin. Ælfric and the early medieval English *Soul and Body* poet describe "wyrmas" (worms) that consume the body after death, connecting the concept of "wyrm" with the mortal body as distinguished from the soul.

Liber Monstrorum (see Section 4) catalogues monsters and marvels in Europe (including several from Greek mythology) as well as Asia. European giants and hybrids occupy specific places, except for a reference to a girl tossed ashore by waves in the west of Europe (Orchard, 1995, I.13). The *Liber* says that Hygelac, gigantic king of the Geats, was buried on an island in the Rhine delta, and Colossus threw himself into the Tiber River while dying of his wounds but was so large he could not be submerged. The island of Sicily is home to Cyclops, and Hercules erected pillars at the entrance to the Mediterranean Sea. In Arcadia a singular monster, hairy all over, lives in a cave and "flammas de pectore euomens" (vomits flames from his breast, I.31). Circe's island in the Mediterranean Sea has lions, bears, and boars, as well as wolves with wild beasts' bodies but human faces (I.41). Like *Beowulf*, the *Liber Monstrorum* combines historical figures with fantastic creatures.

Farther away, Paradise is located far to the east, at the top of medieval maps. Uncultivated and untracked by humans since the expulsion of Adam and Eve, it fits the definition of wilderness. *The Phoenix* locates the legendary bird's home

---

[39] See Brady, 2017; O'Brien O'Keeffe, 2001; and Cohen, 2003, esp. 140–6.

in Paradise "feor heonan / eastdælum on æþelast londa" (far from here, in eastern parts in the holiest of lands, Krapp and Dobbie, 1936, 1b–2). Paradise has woods and plains, but no hills or cliffs; there is never cold, heat, rain, or frost, and the trees always hang with fruit. The Paradise of *Phoenix* cannot be traversed by humans as it is "afyrred . . . / þurh meotudes meaht manfremmendum" (withdrawn from evil-doers through the might of God, 5b–6). The element "man" in "manfremmendum" refers to "sin," but wordplay points to human sinners. Paradise sits on a mesa twelve fathoms higher than the surrounding lands, so that during the great flood it remained untouched by rushing waters. The phoenix originates in Greek mythology but in Christian reinterpretation becomes a symbol of Christ because he periodically dies and is reborn. In *Wonders of the East*, phoenixes are a species (fugel-cynn, Fulk, 2010, 126) rather than the "anhaga" (solitary one, 87) of the poem.

In the poem, the Phoenix grows old and flies from Paradise to "westen" (wilderness, 161). The Old English *Genesis* and *Judith* depict wilderness in terms of mountains and cliffs, but *Phoenix* does not describe the region where the bird takes leadership over other fowl. Each member of the great multitude wishes to serve the Phoenix, suggesting Christians who wish to serve Jesus. The Phoenix abruptly leaves the other birds, which "gesecað Syrwara lond" (seek Syrian land, 166), tying this imaginary space to a real place on a pilgrimage route. The Phoenix then travels westward to a wooded grove, "biholene ond bihydde hæleþa monegum" (concealed and hidden from crowds of men, 17), where he builds a nest which soon bursts into flames, fully consuming him. The ashes congeal into a ball, "æples gelicnes" (like an apple, 230b), from which emerges a worm, which grows into something resembling an "earnes brid" (eagle chick, 235b). From this chick, he grows once again into the Phoenix. The legendary Phoenix's wilderness paradise remains inaccessible to humans but is safely contained in an allegorical frame associated with Jesus that recenters Christians and humans.

"The East"

St. Christopher also originates from far away; he is memorialized in the *Old English Martyrology* entry for April 28 as well as in a prose *Life* in the Beowulf manuscript (Rauer, 2013). The *Martyrology* states that St. Christopher went to Samos, in Greece, "of þære þeod þær men habbað hunda heafod, ond of þære eorðan on ðære æton men hi selfe" (from the people where men have dog's heads, and from the land where men eat one another, 73). Christopher has thick hair, eyes that shine "swa morgensteorra" (like morning-stars) and teeth "swa scearpe swa eoferes tuxas" (as sharp as boar's tusks). Cynocephali, which appear in several early English sources, are unusual among human-animal hybrids, which typically have human heads and upper bodies with animal parts below. The Cotton World Map locates "cinocephales" in the far western edge of Africa, west of the Nile River and near an inscription identifying the continent. The *Wonders of the East* locates them "on þa suð-healfa Egyptana landes" (in the southern half of the Egyptian land, 29), and the *Liber Monstrorum* and the Alexander *Letter* place them in India (*Liber* I.16; *Letter*, Fulk, 2010, 200). The *Passion* in the Beowulf manuscript lacks its opening, which may also have described Christopher as dog-headed.

In addition to its European curiosities, the *Liber Monstrorum* catalogues numerous marvels and monsters outside of Europe, mostly in Asia and occasionally in Africa. A group of people living near the Nile and Brixontes are twelve feet tall and very lean, with long noses and extremely white bodies (I.20). Men with no heads, eyes in their shoulders and the remaining capacities of the head in their breasts live on an island in the Brixontes river (I.24). Non-Europeans are often associated generally with "Asia," "India," or "the East," rather than with a particular location. A man with two heads and four hands is "in Asia natum" (born in Asia, I.8). People covered with hair and bristles who eat only raw fish live in India (I.15). Men and women of great beauty (I.26), people of normal size but whose eyes "sicunt laterna lucent" (glow like lanterns, I.36), and people who grow to fifteen feet tall with bodies white like marble and ears like baskets (I.43) live in "Oriente" (the East, I.26).

Many monsters are characterized specifically as female, as opposed to other "races" whose gender is not mentioned (see Section 4). A group of twelve-foot-tall women with marble-like skin, hair that reaches nearly to the ground, cows' tails, and camels' feet live near the Red Sea (I.28). Gorgons "in monstruosa mulierum natura" (of women's monstrous nature) who turn men to stone live near Mount Atlas in Libya (I.38). Women born near the mountains of Armenia have long beards and are covered with hair and breed tigers and leopards instead of dogs (I.22). Harpies, birds with the faces of young women who steal people's food with their claws, live on islands in the Ionian Sea (I.44). A group of women who sleep on iron beds in the underworld have snakes on their heads instead of hair, among them blue snakes that "uesanam discordiam scatebant" (swarm in wild disagreement, I.45).

In addition to descriptions of real people and places (Section 4), the Alexander *Letter* relates numerous anecdotes about fabulous creatures. Alexander and his army encounter enormous and horned serpents of various colors, some with three-pronged tongues that breathe fire and poison (115–21), white lions the size of bulls (123–4), unmeasurably large boars (125), bats the size of doves with human teeth (126–7), and mice the size of foxes (137).

Alexander also encounters humans with unexpected quantities of hair who are nine feet tall and catch and eat whales (196–9).

The only place that Alexander treats with respect is the Grove of the Sun and the Moon, the last place he visits and the most difficult to find, where he travels with a fraction of his army. He is greeted by a bishop, 300 years old, ten feet tall, and entirely black except for white teeth who is clothed in "wildeora fellum" (the pelts of wild animals), and wears earrings "of mænigfealdan gim-cynne geworhte" (made of many kinds of gems, 241–5). This is a kind of earthly paradise: the bishop tells Alexander that in this land, "næfre … regnes dropa ne cwome ne fugel ne wildeor, ne nænig ætern wyrm" (there never came a drop of rain, nor fowl, nor wild animals, nor any poisonous snake, 236). The bishop tells Alexander that the trees can perceive the thoughts of any person looking at them and answer questions. They tell Alexander that he will be betrayed by a close associate within two years, and that he will die "nalles mid iserne acweald swa ðu wenst, ac mid atre" (not killed by iron, as you believe, but by poison, 283). The trees refuse to give him any further information, because "þu ða wyrde oncyrrest" (then you would turn fate aside, 283).

Wonders of the East catalogues fantastical creatures often similar to those in the *Liber* and the *Letter*.[40] There are rams as big as oxen (5), ants as big as dogs (34), animals with parts from a variety of known creatures (53–4), and dragons (57). Human figures in *Wonders* include people two and three times the expected size (45, 50), people with manes like lions (47), men without heads whose faces are on their chests (55), donkey-human hybrids (53–4), bearded women who hunt (88–9), and a group of women with boar's tusks, oxtails, and camel's feet (90–3). Mittman and Kim (2013) point out a passage in *Wonders* mentioning Alexander by name, and the contrast between his slaughter of monstrous, sexually transgressive women and admiration of the men who are generous in giving gifts of women to Alexander and other outsiders.[41]

Whereas we only have one manuscript of most Old English poems, including *Beowulf*, *Wonders* was popular enough to have been copied three times: in Latin, in Old English, and with both languages. All three versions are illustrated, providing physical depictions of humans, animals, and monsters that sometimes echo but also sometimes conflict with the verbal descriptions. Other than drawings of rivers, mountains, and cities, the only animate figure on the Cotton World Map is a lion.[42] However, the drawings in the manuscripts of *Wonders* often bear surprising similarity to those appearing on the thirteenth-century *Hereford Mappa Mundi* (see Foys, Crossley, and Wacha, 2020), suggesting continuity in the ideas

---

[40] See Section 4 for a discussion of the titular "East."

[41] For more on the women Alexander kills and those he leaves alive, see Discenza, 2017, 94–5.

[42] But see Foys, Crossley, and Wacha, 2020, for Peter Barber's reading of two fighting figures in Cornwall.

about people, animals, monsters and places outside of Europe. The ideas current in early medieval England were part of a broader European textual culture that persisted into the later Middle Ages and influenced the "invention of race" (Heng, 2018; see Section 4) in the thirteenth century.

Mermedonia

Mermedonia is very far away across the sea, but otherwise its location is unclear in early English sources.[43] The story of Andrew rescuing Matthew from the Mermedonians exists in two Old English versions, the poetic *Andreas* and prose *Life of Andrew* in the Blickling Homily (18 in Kelly, 2003). When the poem opens, St. Matthew has gone to preach but has been imprisoned by the Mermedonian people, cannibals who plan to eat him along with other prisoners. God instructs Andrew, who is in Greece, to go and rescue Matthew, but he protests, citing the great distance, cold water, and dangerous seas (*Andreas*, Krapp, 1932, 190–202). After God rebukes him, Andrew finds a ship captained by men Andrew thinks are ordinary sailors but are actually two angels and Jesus, who tries to dissuade Andrew from the journey because Mermedonia is too far "ofer widne mære" (across the wide sea, 283). When Andrew falls asleep, the angels transport him and his men "ofer yða geþræc" (over the violence of the waves, 823). The poem insists on the materiality of the waves and the water, but Andrew arrives in Mermedonia only through divine intervention, transported as if by magic across both great distance and insurmountable storm. The poem then supplies geographical details about Mermedonia. Andrew awakes before "burggeatum" (city gates, 840a) and sees mountains, towers, walls, and tiled buildings. As in *Beowulf*, *Judith*, and *Genesis*, wilderness in the poetic *Andreas* is described in terms of stone and cliff. Yet here wilderness meets the peak of civilization: stone and tile buildings and towers were known in England mostly from Roman ruins. The Homily includes no details about the city, though its opening has been lost. Andrew and his thegns go to the prison, where Andrew's prayers cause the prison guards to fall dead so that he can free Matthew as well as all the other prisoners.

Andrew goes into the city to wait for the Mermedonians to discover the empty prison and the loss of their food. The Mermedonians, prompted by the devil, torture Andrew. In the Homily, they drag him through the city streets by a rope around the neck. The poem broadens the scene of Andrew's torture to include the wilderness seen in his first view of the island. The Mermedonians drag Andrew "æfter dunscræfum, / ymb stanhleoðo" (through hill-caves, near rocky slopes, 1232b–1233a), and finally back into the walled city, over "enta

---

[43] Brooks, 1961, describes the location as given in other sources, xxvii–xxx, but neither the poem nor the Blickling Homily as extant give these details.

ærgeweorc, innan burgum, / stræte stanfage" (old giants' work inside the walled town's stone-paved streets, 1235–1236a). Andrew is further harried by a cold night punctuated by snow and hail showers described as "hare hildstapan" (hoary battle-steppers, 1258). The city and wilderness are passive objects used in Andreas' torture, but the weather participates actively. Earlier, the stormy sea had been commanded by Jesus, who whipped up the waters and calmed them at his will to test Andrew and his companions, but here weather seems independently hostile, as in the Exeter Book "storm" Riddles (Estes, 2021). Andrew takes control of the city and causes a stone idol to release a flood of water that threatens to drown the Mermedonians; the worst are swept to hell but the majority convert to Christianity. The fantasy of the conversion of all the Mermedonian heathens echoes the scene at the end of *Elene* when all the Jews become Christian.

Conclusion

Texts that were translated and adapted into Old English depict a variety of imagined landscapes, animals, monsters, and people, both close to home and unfathomably far away. The interlaced depictions of gender, monstrosity, and religious difference highlight the monastic contexts in which virtually all Old English literature was written. Writers are fascinated by the worlds they imagine, deep under the water and far away, displacing everyday fears of illness, famine, and local conflicts onto fabulous and monstrous creatures elsewhere and, unfortunately, setting the stage for later travelers to meet ordinary humans in distant places and interpret them as monstrous. At the same time, the texts offer some containment of the threats by naming and classifying them.

6 Hell, Purgatory, and Heaven

Early medieval English people translated and adapted Latin texts including the Bible, commentaries, and sermons, in developing their ideas about what came after death. They viewed heaven and hell as real places, not as fantastic or figurative, and they expected eventually to find themselves in one of them. Mary Rambaran-Olm notes that in early Jewish tradition, Sheol, an underworld of permanent separation from God without punishment or reward, was the destination after death for all. Later Jewish thinkers wrote that the wicked would be punished in Gehenna, and some thought that a messiah would reward believers with resurrection (2014, 35–7). Christians then elaborated their own notions of hell for sinners, and heaven, opened by Jesus, for righteous believers (37–8). Building on this tradition, authors described hell and heaven variously as natural environments, constructed ones, or both. They resemble places on Earth, albeit in extreme versions. Hell often appears as an awful region of ice and fiery darkness; heaven frequently appears as a glorious landscape of beauty, music, and light. In some Old English texts, hell is a perversion of the hall and heaven a perfect version of it. The terrors of hell are inverted in the glories of heaven: stench and cries below contrast directly with pleasant fragrances, music, and joy above.

Purgatory seems not to have been fully established among Christians in early medieval England. Some writers refer to practices related to purgatory such as praying, having masses said, and giving alms for the dead, but they take the perspective of the living who engage in these practices rather than of the souls that reside there. Where purgatory is depicted, it is, like hell, a place of suffering, different in that this torment cleanses the soul of sin and its effects so that the soul will eventually go to heaven.

Heaven

Portrayals of heaven are plentiful. The word could be used in multiple ways, as in present-day English: it can mean the physical space above us, more distant realms beyond sight, and a spiritual place that for some has no reality and for others is incorporeal. Early medieval English writers sometimes gave more precise accounts of the location of heaven than of hell, although they did not always agree on all details. Heaven is as real and physical as Earth, and may appear as a beautiful landscape, a glorious city, or a hall.

Above Earth is the atmosphere; above that, the moon, planets, sun, and most distant stars; and beyond all that lies heaven, the kingdom of God. The Old English *Boethius* imagines a journey in which the protagonist has feathers to fly above the air and beyond the sun and stars. Saturn is "eallisig" (all icy) and wanders farther than any other stars (Godden and Irvine, 2009, 36.49–50). After the narrator has passed "bufan þam swiftan rodore" (above the swiftly moving heaven), he can receive the true light where the most powerful king reigns (36.50–53). The passage stays within the realm of the corporeal; the light of heaven is as physical as Saturn's chill. If people could fly, they might eventually reach the kingdom of God. Visual art conveys this same physicality in depictions of Christ ascending into heaven. He does not simply vanish into a burst of light or even a cloud; instead, his feet are shown rising above the Earth, a physical ascent to a physical location. Sometimes, the feet are the only part of him that can be seen, a representation known as the Disappearing Christ that became common in eleventh-century England.[44]

---

[44] See, for instance, the illustrations in Calum Cockburn, "The Ascension in Anglo-Saxon England," *Medieval Manuscripts Blog*, The British Library, January 31, 2019, https://blogs .bl.uk/digitisedmanuscripts/2019/01/the-ascension-in-anglo-saxon-england.html.

Heaven's beauty results directly from God's presence, as *The Phoenix* proclaims: "Heofonas sindon / fægre gefylled, fæder ælmihtig, / ealra þrymma þrym" (The heavens are filled with beauty, Father Almighty, glory of all glories, 626–9). Heaven's beauty is inseparable from God's in Old English texts. *Christ and Satan* combines pastoral beauty with buildings: heaven is "fægere land þonne þeos folde seo; / is þær wlitig and wynsum, wæstmas scinað, / beorhte ofer burgum" (a more beautiful land than is this earth; there it is gorgeous and lovely, fruits shine bright over the enclosures, 212–14). Ælfric normally offers few geographical or architectural details, but he makes an exception for *Saint Thomas*. Thomas is an architect and builder, and Christ arranges for Abbanes, the steward of the king of India, to hire him to build the king's palace. Thomas describes his work, including a foundation that lasts forever, walls that never sink, perfect windows, and divine light; "hire hrof ofer-stihð / ealle gebytlu and bið utan fæger/ and swa-þeah wlitigre þæt weorc wiðinnan" (its roof surpasses all buildings and is beautiful outside, and yet more beautiful is the work within, Clayton and Mullins, 2019, vol. 3, 71–3). Abbanes thinks Thomas speaks about his earthly works, but Christian audiences recognize that he simultaneously describes building the kingdom of heaven.

For Ælfric, the construction of heaven is no mere metaphor. The king of India imprisons Thomas for converting his people to Christianity, but then the king's beloved brother Gad dies. He goes to hell and then to heaven before returning to life. He says that he has seen replicas of Thomas' construction. Angels explain that "þa scinendan gebytlu" (the shining buildings) are indeed the ones Thomas built on Earth for the king, and Gad adds, "Ic wiscte þa þæt ic moste on þam mæran huse / huru durewerd beon" (I wished then that I might be a doorkeeper in that splendid house, 141 and 144–5). Thomas' work on Earth creates such beauty in heaven that a man of royal family would be happy to be a doorkeeper there. Ælfric writes that Gad and his brother must buy (*bigst*, 149; *gebicgan*, 177 and 178; *geceapode*, 187) their places in heaven through conversion and devotion to God, and Thomas explains that the Savior has built uncountable dwellings in heaven, to be purchased by faith (184–7). Ælfric's architectural focus brings home to audiences the splendor of heaven as Roman architecture (39, 91) built with precious materials such as fine wood, marble, and jewels.

Even more than beauty, light is associated with heaven. *Andreas* coins two compounds for "heaven-light," *heofonleoht* and *heofonleoma* (Krapp, 1932, 974, 838). Four poems have a compound for "heaven-bright," comparing the brightness of heaven to earthly things.[45] The light of heaven is among the greatest losses to the fallen angels (*Genesis* 83–6, *Christ and Satan* 140–4, both in Krapp, 1931).

---

[45] *Andreas* 1018 and 1269, *Order of the World* 73 (Krapp and Dobbie, 1936), *Exodus* 78 (Krapp, 1931), and *The Old English Boethius*, Meter 23.3 (Godden and Irvine, 2009).

Heaven stimulates other senses too. In a vision of the afterlife in Bede's *Ecclesiastical History*, Dryhthelm of Coldingham only comes to its outskirts, but he remarks on the wonderful smell, the field of flowers and "cantatium dulcissimam" (the sweetest singing, Colgrave and Mynors, 1969, V.12). Similarly, Ælfric writes that at the Saint Martin's death, Bishop Severinus of Cologne hears "hludne sang on heofonum" (loud song in the heavens, Clayton and Mullins, 2019, vol. 3, *Saint Martin*, 1387) and concludes that the angels are singing as they carry Martin to heaven and welcome him in – so loudly that he could hear them on Earth (1385–1402). The word *dream* can mean both "joy" and "music" in Old English; it appears more than fifty times in the *Old English Corpus* in conjunction with forms of *heofon*, and many passages allow for both meanings.

Hell

Early medieval English writers imagined hell as a place deep under the Earth, dark yet lit by flames; they also emphasized darkness and cold alternating with searing heat. In poetry, hell can be a hall or a home, a macabre parody of safe space. Hell's fires appear in several Old English poems, a dozen of Ælfric's homilies and saints' lives, and many homilies by others. In the Old English poem *Genesis*, hell is *synnihte* (everlasting night, 42). The poet repeatedly uses forms of *sweart* and *þystro*, both meaning "dark." The poem *Christ and Satan* calls hell "ðeostræ ham" (the home of darkness, 38). Homilies and lives of saints by Ælfric, Wulfstan, and anonymous writers often pair "sweart" and "þyst-" with "hell" or describe it as a place without light. The combination of subterranean location, darkness, and flames led the monk Willibald to climb Vulcano, known as the Hell of Theodoric, to see what hell would be like; massed ashes kept him from reaching the top (Holder-Egger 1887, 101.30–102.2; trans. Talbot, 1954, 171; see Section 2).

Other early English literary depictions place hell deep beneath the Earth's surface, following classical writers who conceived of an afterlife in the underworld and Christian writers who wrote of a descent into hell. In the poem *Genesis*, before the creation of Earth, rebellious angels fall so far from heaven that it takes them three nights and days to reach hell (306–7). The word *grund* (abyss) and the compound *hellegrund* (abyss or depths of hell) repeatedly describe hell in the poems *Genesis* and *Christ and Satan* and homilies by Ælfric and Wulfstan.

In addition to depths and burning, some early English writers imagine hell as a place of extreme cold. In Felix's *Life of St. Guthlac*, demons snatch the saint and take him to the mouth of hell to terrify him; he sees there "Non solum enim fluctuantium flammarum ignivomos gurgites illic … immo etiam sulphurei glaciali grandine mixti vortiges" (not only whirlpools vomiting waves of flame there . . . but also frozen hail mixed with sulfurous currents, Colgrave 1956, 31). The Old English *Genesis* says hell is "geondfolen fyre and færcyle, / rece and reade lege" (filled all around with fire and extreme cold, smoke and red flame, 43–4) and later juxtaposes fire with "forst fyrnum cald" (torturously cold frost, 449). In *Christ and Satan*, Satan observes, "hat and ceald hwilum mencgað" (hot and cold sometimes mix, 131); later, the narrator says Satan can expect nothing but "cyle and fyr" (cold and fire, 334b).

A handful of homilies associate hell with both darkness and monsters. Most notably, the Homily *To Sanctae Michaheles Mæssan* ends with a moment taken from the Vision of St. Paul, an apocryphal but popular account of St. Paul's vision of heaven and hell. In this brief passage, Paul sees icy groves by a hoary stone under which all the waters descend, and "þystrogenipo, ond under þæm stane was niccra eardung ond wearga" (dark miasmas, and under the stone was the lair of water monsters and evil creatures, Kelly, 2003, lines 200–1). Souls hang from the icy groves like bodies tied by their hands, and devils resembling water monsters pull on them until they can seize them (201–7). In *Beowulf*, Grendel's mother's mere resembles this conception of hell, with icy woods, a hoary stone, and waters full of monsters. Hell is in the north in the Blickling Homily and Felix's *Life of St. Guthlac* (chapter 31), probably following Isaiah 14:13, which Christians read as a depiction of Lucifer plotting to establish his throne in the north.

In early medieval English texts, souls in hell feel temperature the way their bodies would and experience demons and worms eating them as if their souls were their own decaying bodies. In Ælfric's *Saints Julian and Basilissa*, the early Christian martyr Julian memorably tells his tormentor Martianus that the latter will go to hell and will encounter "undeadlic wyrm, / þe eowre lic-haman cywð and ge þeah ne sweltað, / ac bið æfre se lic-hama geedniwod to ðam witum" (immortal worms, which will chew your body and yet you will not die, but always your body will be restored for that torture, Clayton and Mullins, 2019, vol. 3, *Saints Julian and Basilissa*, 386–8). Old English *wyrm* can mean worm, snake, or dragon, depending on context; here, any of the translations would fit. *Christ and Satan* adds venom to the *wrym*'s torments (39–40 and 127–8).

The horror of these tortures deepens with the poetic idea that hell is a hall or even a home. In the seventh century, the English began to build large halls that served literally and symbolically as images of community, strength, and protection at the center of settlements. Warriors gathered, ate, and slept in such spaces, as in *Beowulf*: Grendel's terror and later his mother's result partly from their ability to kill in what should be an intimate and safe place. Hell as hall, then, is a perversion of an ideal (Discenza, 2017, 179–93 and 217–18). In *Judith*, some warriors are transported to a grotesque "wyrmsele" (worm-hall, Dobbie, 1953, 119) and in *Christ and Satan*, hell is a windy hall (35 and 319) with a poisoned floor (39–40 and 317). The fallen angels "in helle ham staðeledon" (established a home in hell, 25), and it is simultaneously "atole scref" (a dark grave, 26). The Old English poems *Genesis*, *Guthlac*, *Juliana*, and *Judgment Day I* also depict hell as home.

Hell sometimes appears as a fortress or city: what should be a paragon of human achievement and safety has been perverted into the worst of tortures by its denizens' sins (Discenza, 2017, 193–219). The poem *Descent into Hell* describes hell as a *burg* (stronghold or city) with walls and gates (33–57).[46] Ælfric reads Babylon and Gaza as images of hell: in an Easter homily, Samson becomes a prefiguration of Christ, and "Seo burh gaza getacnode helle" (The city Gaza represents hell, Clemoes, 1997, I.15.163–4); in a homily for the second Sunday after Epiphany, Babylon prefigures hell (Godden, 1979, II.4.233–4).

Bede's Afterlife

One of the rare descriptions of purgatory, along with a detailed account of hell and a glimpse of heaven, appears in Bede's account of Dryhthelm's vision. Notably, however, Bede does not use the word "purgatory," or any equivalent, merely describing the place. Dryhthelm dies, or appears to, and sees "uallem multae latitudinis ac profunditatis, infinitae autem longitudinis" (a very wide and deep valley of infinite length, Colgrave and Mynors, 1969, V.12). One side has terrible flames; the other is "furenti grandine ac frigore niuium omnia perflante atque uerrente non minus intolerabile" (no less intolerable for the raging hail and cold snow blowing and scouring everything). Souls change sides frequently, seeking relief that does not come. Dryhthelm thinks it is hell, but his guide corrects him, explaining that this place is for souls who repented and confessed shortly before death. Repentance saved them from hell, but they suffer purgatory because they had no time to change their ways in life. Prayers, charity, and fasting by the living may free them before the Last Judgment, according to Bede (V.12).

Authors do not all agree about whether purgatory is a place or a state of being, or how it looked and felt (Foxhall Forbes, 2010, 668; 2013, 203). Few writers from early medieval England refer to purgatory. It is not clear whether Wulfstan, for instance, took it for granted and focused on the Last Judgment in his writings, or did not believe that purgatory existed (Foxhall Forbes, 2013, 17–18 and 207). In addition to Bede, English writers including Boniface (670s–754) and Ælfric of Eynsham (ca. 950–ca. 1010) made references to a place where souls suffered to be purged of sins before going to heaven.

From this liminal space, Bede's Dryhthelm continues to hell, "uidi subito ante nos obscurari incipere loca, et tenebris omnia repleri" (Suddenly I saw the

---

[46] Or *John the Baptist's Prayer*: see Rambaran-Olm, 2014, especially 53–8.

places before us begin to dim and darkness filled everything, *Ecclesiastical History* V.12). At first, he can only see his guide; in the darkness, "subito apparent ante nos crebri flammarum tetrarum globi ascendentes quasi de puteo magno rursumque decidentes in eundum" (suddenly before us appeared balls of foul flame, frequently rising as if from a great pit and falling into it again). His guide vanishes, and Dryhthelm realizes that human souls are in the flames. Dryhthelm emphasizes repeatedly the "fetor incomparabilis" (incomparable stench), a detail found in some homilies but not in Old English poetry. Dryhthelm also describes the souls' weeping and the exultantly cackling evil spirits who thrust souls into the pit. The spirits threaten Dryhthelm, but his guide reappears and puts them to flight, then leads Dryhthelm out of this space, which he later explains was the "os gehennae" (the mouth of hell, V.12).

Bede includes a second space that is neither heaven nor hell, atypical among early medieval English writers; it resembles the portion of the Greek underworld where good people spend eternity. Dryhthelm sees a place with "multo maiorem luminis gratiam quam prius" (a much more grace-filled light than before, V.12) and mistakes this for heaven: the singing is *dulcissimam* (sweetest), the smell is *miri* (wondrous), the light is *eximia* (exceptional), and the young people are *pulcherrimam* (most beautiful, V.12; see Kabir, 2001). Yet his guide tells him that this too is a waiting place: the souls of the good who do not need purgation but are not yet holy enough to enter heaven wait in this pleasant space until Judgment Day (494). In addition to Bede's popular Latin text, this vision was transmitted in the Old English *Bede* or in Ælfric's rendering for his homily "Alia visio" (Another Vision, Godden, 1979, II.21). Ælfric follows Bede in describing four distinct spaces (hell, purgatory, antechamber of heaven, and the unseen heaven beyond), but he downplays the glory of the pleasant interim place to make it more earthly than heavenly (Foxhall Forbes, 2010, 675–8).

Conclusion

Early English readers and writers did not all have exactly the same notions of hell, purgatory, and heaven. Some make no mention of purgatory and may have believed in a simple division between heaven and hell; some, such as Bede, may have envisioned more than three locations in the afterlife. Early medieval English writers disagree on some conditions in these places. Hell may be full of fire, or both fire and ice; it may be lightless or lit by flames. Hell and heaven may be portrayed as natural landscapes, built environments, or a combination. Where the early medieval English do show consistency is in representing them as physical places, not mere abstractions or metaphors. Hell, heaven, and sometimes purgatory are as real as London or Rome. Unlike London or Rome, however, at least one of these would be the destination for each person.

Conclusions

The people of early medieval England translated, adapted, and wrote a variety of different texts – secular and religious poetry, homilies, saints' lives, histories and chronicles – in which they described their place in the rest of the world. These texts participated in a broader European, Christian textual culture that continued to be disseminated in England during the later medieval and early modern periods, thus influencing how colonizers encountered other parts of the world and the people who lived in them. Today, these ideas still influence how some English-speaking people in the British Isles, North America, and Australia, among others, understand themselves, nationally and globally, in the context of race, religion, ethnicity, and gender.

It is crucial, therefore, to realize that early medieval England was far more diverse and better connected to a broader world than scholars and novelists, filmmakers and video game designers often imagine. Many people had roots in other places or ethnic groups: Germanic and Scandinavian, North African, Celtic, and Greek. Many identified in multiple ways: Jutish descent, Kentish woman, English. Their geographies were more often verbal than visually mapped, and while they could be very detailed in describing local property lines in charters or locating city gates, they often did not conceptualize larger entities in terms of hard boundaries. Scandinavians were familiar to the English as allies and family members but also as mortal enemies. The English shared the British Isles with Celts but often distinguished themselves from them in ways that alternately praised or diminished the others: the Welsh could be scholars or slaves; the Scots and Irish could be pious and learned or deviants from Roman Church practices. In the early medieval period, "Anglian" (the word that evolves into the modern "English") referred only to one of the peoples who spoke Old English in the British Isles. Exogamous family relationships among all these peoples meant that "English" (a descriptor adopted late) was never a simple identity.

England's people maintained ties with Scandinavia and mainland Europe through kinship and religious connections, trade, and military alliances. West Francia contributed to the conversion of the English to Christianity, and the English reciprocated by sending religious men and women to established houses there, as well as missionaries to what would become the Low Countries and Germany. Rome was a religious and cultural center for the early English, and travelers went as far as Byzantium. The Iberian Peninsula was physically closer but perhaps subjectively more distant: writers recall past Christian heretics and Christian saints, and they characterize its present in terms of Muslims and danger. Texts about distant places in Europe show significant interest in peoples and customs but little engagement with landscape or buildings. Ties to mainland Europe would grow stronger with the Norman Conquest, as the new ruling class of England retained holdings in Normandy and maintained networks established before they moved to England.

When writing about the area around Jerusalem, English authors gave more attention to physical settings. In poetry, saints' lives, and travelogues, writers demonstrated fascination with lands featured in the Bible, especially the Christian New Testament. Jerusalem and its environs function as the Earth's physical and spiritual center in many texts. Yet the curiosity of, say, Wulfstan about the funeral customs of the Ests (Section 2) does not carry over into any interest in the beliefs and customs of Jews and Muslims. English Christian writers tended to divide Jews into two: a few exemplary Jews from the time before Jesus appear positively, as children of Israel and the chosen ones of God, while other Jews are portrayed as wilful sinners, knowing Jewish law but often disregarding it. Both groups are projected into the present, with idealized Jews conceived as forebears of Christianity, and other Jews identified with Gospel and postbiblical Jews who were blamed for Jesus' death and reviled because they did not share the Christian faith. Similarly, Muslims are treated as bad Christians, rather than followers of a separate faith. While missionaries sought to convert European peoples with whom they perceived a common ancestry, pilgrims to Palestine seem to have had no interest converting Jews or Muslims. Not long after the Norman Conquest, this disinterest would turn to active violence as English people embraced the First Crusade. The *Peterborough Chronicle* recounts that because of Pope Urban's call, "ferde unarimedlic folc mid wifan 7 cildan to þi þet hi upon hæðene þeodan winnan woldan" (countless people went with women and children so that they could fight against the heathen people, Irvine, 2004, 1096).

Ambivalence marks English attitudes to biblical lands, the rest of Asia, and Africa. Trade with both continents has left evidence in archaeology and the documentary record, while the Old English *Orosius*, like its Latin source, presents portions of them as simply part of a wider world, as is Europe. Bede's *Ecclesiastical History* and the Old English *Soliloquies* depict Augustine of Hippo and Archbishop Hadrian as African men of great learning and piety who influenced English culture. *The Letter of Alexander to Aristotle* has moments in this vein, with dazzling cities and a bishop in India, but more often it depicts the people of India and beyond as uncultured and even monstrous. *The Wonders of the East* and *Liber Monstrorum* do even more to distance the inhabitants of Africa and Asia from the English and other Europeans.

People, animals, and plants in these works are described as vastly different from those in Europe. Writers connect race to skin color or hair, and they link it to transgressed gender norms (men who behave like women and vice versa) and appalling behavior, particularly cannibalism.

While *The Letter* often places extraordinary people and animals in knowable places, *Wonders* and *Liber* transport audiences to imagined lands whose locations cannot be described or mapped. The imagined inhabitants in texts such as *Beowulf* and *Guthlac* – hybrid human-animals, demons, the Grendelkin, dragons, and cannibals – sometimes seem to move outside of normal space. In the views of English people, differences of religion, race, gender definitions, and behavior seem to set outsiders apart, and they describe the places and the people who live in them in terms of wonder and often terror. While race as a category became more solidly established only later in the Middle Ages, the early English characterizations of evil descendants of Cain and diabolical Britons living in their midst, as well as monstrous humans in places far away, shows problematic stereotyping of "others" already well underway.

Individual English writers and readers may or may not have believed that these imagined peoples existed. Most of them probably regarded hell and heaven as real places, with some believing in purgatory as well, yet they needed imagination to convey the qualities of these spaces. The horror of hell comes in visions or by analogy: the frigid wilderness of the vision of St. Paul; the alternating hot and cold of Dryhthelm's experience; the volcano said to be like hell; or a perverted hall, with none of the safety and community such a place should offer. Some writers see purgatory as a hell-like space but temporary, before a soul goes to heaven; Bede adds a kind of waiting space, far more beautiful but not yet the fullness of heaven, in a passage that confused even his contemporaries. Limbo and places for virtuous pagans such as we see in Dante's *Inferno* do not appear in early medieval English literature. Heaven is a delightful landscape, a perfect hall, or a city full of beautiful buildings.

The descriptions of volcanoes, the gates and churches of Jerusalem, and the combination of wilderness and urban architecture in *Andreas* stand out for their rare interest in non-English landscapes, both natural and built. Attention to the boundaries of different lands or their exact spatial relationships is rare; travelogues do not help readers get to the places listed, and maps are ways of conceptualizing the world more than aids to navigation.

As did the people of early medieval England, many today divide people along geographical lines, though today we insist more on physical borders. Concern about differences in religion, sex and gender, skin color, hair, and customs remain and even intensify in later eras. The balance of power in England's missionary work shifted considerably in later centuries: where early English evangelists might have some backing from the Franks, they came with little or no military force and focused on mainland European relatives. After the Norman Conquest, England gained a sizable Jewish population, which it sought to control, sometimes pressured to convert, and ultimately expelled, after a number of local massacres of Jews. The First Crusade drew contingents from England and Normandy, and more English joined later in the Crusades before their participation began to wane again. The early modern era saw missionaries from England backed by military might that enforced specific varieties of Christianity around the globe.

Also after the Conquest, a substantial group of surviving English nobles joined the Varangian Guard, a force that served the Byzantine emperor, serving alongside Rus' and Scandinavian soldiers. Historical reports attest the existence of a *Nova Anglia*, a "New England" established in the Crimea by *Saxi*, "Saxons" or "English," who named a city London. Traces of it appear in maps as late as the sixteenth century, though its exact location is now uncertain, and not all scholars agree about its historicity or how long it may have lasted (Pelteret, 2014, 96–110; Green, 2015). The English had never been confined to their island, and the post-Conquest period saw the start of colonial expansion in Wales, which later extended to Scotland and Ireland, and eventually beyond the British Isles to Africa, India, China, and the Americas.

The early medieval English came from many places and did not immediately form a unified land. While conceptions of the rest of the world changed over time and varied among individual writers, these early authors and audiences constantly engaged with worlds within and outside their own island. Their position near the edge of the known world meant that later English expansion around the globe was neither inevitable nor obvious, but the attitudes shown in this Element would continue and develop in later periods. English desire for connections abroad grew even stronger in the centuries after the Conquest. Conflicting attitudes toward Africa and Asia as places that produced learning and luxury goods but that were also homes to people who were conceived of as profoundly different from, and often inferior to, the English, played out in exploration and conquests with lasting consequences for people around the globe. Conceptions of heaven and hell already present in this early era helped propel missions inseparable from the conquests and exploitation of colonized peoples. Those conflicting attitudes, however, offer possibilities for rethinking even now. The hybrid heritage of the English people and the impact of Celtic, Roman, North African, and Greek cultures on early medieval English culture should impel us to seek more openness in early medieval English studies and more connections with other places and fields. We have much yet to learn.

Bibliography

Primary Texts

Anlezark, Daniel, ed. and trans. (2009) *The Old English Dialogues of Solomon and Saturn*. Cambridge: Brewer.

Baker, Peter, ed. (2000) *The Anglo-Saxon Chronicle: A Collaborative Edition* vol. 8: *MS F*. Cambridge: Brewer.

Bately, Janet, ed. (1980) *The Old English Orosius*. Early English Text Society supplementary series no. 6. Oxford: Oxford University Press.

  (1986) *The Anglo-Saxon Chronicle: A Collaborative Edition* vol. 3: *MS A*. Cambridge: Brewer.

Clayton, Mary, and Hugh Magennis. (1994) *The Old English Lives of St. Margaret*. Cambridge: Cambridge University Press.

Clayton, Mary, and Juliet Mullins, ed. and trans. (2019) *Ælfric: Lives of Saints*. 3 vols. Dumbarton Oaks Medieval Library 58–60. Harvard, MA: Harvard University Press.

Clemoes, Peter. (1997) *Ælfric's Catholic Homilies: The First Series: Text*. Early English Text Society supplementary series no. 17. Oxford: Oxford University Press.

Colgrave, Bertram, ed. and trans. (1956) *Felix's Life of Saint Guthlac*. Cambridge: Cambridge University Press.

Colgrave, Bertram, and Roger Aubrey Baskerville Mynors, eds. (1969) *Bede's Ecclesiastical History of the English People*. Oxford: Clarendon.

Crawford, Samuel John, ed. (1922) *The Old English Version of the Heptateuch, Ælfric's Treatise on the Old and New Testament and His Preface to Genesis*. Early English Text Society original series 160. London: Oxford University Press.

Cubbin, Geoffrey P., ed. (1996) *The Anglo-Saxon Chronicle: A Collaborative Edition* vol. 5: *MS D*. Cambridge: Brewer.

Dobbie, Elliott Van Kirk, ed. (1942) *The Anglo-Saxon Minor Poems*. Anglo-Saxon Poetic Records 6. New York: Columbia University Press.

  (1953) *Beowulf and Judith*. Anglo-Saxon Poetic Records 4. New York: Columbia University Press.

Estes, Heide. (2012) Anglo-Saxon Biblical Lore: An Edition. *English Studies* 93(6): 623–51.

Ferrante, Joan, ed. (2014) *Epistolae: Medieval Latin Women's Letters*. Columbia University Libraries. https://doi.org/10.7916/RK1E-8X32.

Foys, Martin, Cat Crossley, and Heather Wacha, eds. (2020) *Virtual Mappa* 2 0. https://sims2.digitalmappa.org/36.

Fraipont, Jean, ed. (1965) *Bedae Venerabilis De locis sanctis. Itineraria et alia geographica*. Corpus Christianorum Series Latina 155. Brepols: Turnhout: 245–80.

Fulk, Robert D., ed. and trans. (2010) *The Beowulf Manuscript: Complete Texts and the Fight at Finnsburg*. Cambridge, MA: Harvard University Press.

Fulk, Robert D., Robert E. Bjork, and John D. Niles, eds. (2008) *Klaeber's Beowulf and the Fight at Finnsburg*. 4th ed. Toronto: University of Toronto Press.

Godden, Malcolm. (1979) *Ælfric's Catholic Homilies: The Second Series: Text*. Early English Text Society supplementary series no. 5. Oxford: Oxford University Press.

Godden, Malcolm, and Susan Irvine, with Mark Griffith and Rohini Jayatilaka. (2009) *The Old English Boethius: An Edition of the Old English Versions of Boethius's De Consolatione Philosophiae*. 2 vols. Oxford: Oxford University Press.

Hecht, H., ed. (1900–7, repr. 1965) *Bischof Wærferths von Worcester Übersetzung der Dialoge Gregors des Grossen*. Leipzig; repr. Darmstadt: Wissenschaftliche Buchgesellschaft.

Hill, Joyce, ed. (1983) *Old English Minor Heroic Poems*. Durham and St Andrews: Universities of Durham and St Andrews.

Holder-Egger, O., ed. (1887) Hygeburg: *Vita Willibaldi episcopi Eichstetensis*. MGH Scriptores 15. Berlin: 86–106.

Irvine, Susan, ed. (2004) *The Anglo-Saxon Chronicle: A Collaborative Edition* vol. 7: *MS E*. Cambridge: Brewer.

Jones, Charles W., ed. (1977) *Bedae Venerabilis Opera*. Pars VI: *Opera Didascalica 2*. Corpus Christianorum Series Latina 123B. Turnhout: Brepols.

Kelly, Richard J., ed. and trans. (2003) *The Blickling Homilies: Edition and Translation*. London: Continuum.

Keynes, Simon, and Michael Lapidge, trans. (1983) *Alfred the Great: Asser's Life of King Alfred and Other Contemporary Sources*. New York: Penguin.

Knock, Ann. (1981) "Wonders of the East: A Synoptic Edition of the Letter of Pharaswines and the Old English and Old Picard Translation." PhD thesis, Birkbeck College, London.

Kramer, Johanna, Hugh Magennis, and Robin Norris, eds. and trans. (2020) *Anonymous Old English Lives of Saints*. Dumbarton Oaks Medieval Library 63. Harvard, MA: Harvard University Press.

Krapp, George Philip, ed. (1931) *The Junius Manuscript*. Anglo-Saxon Poetic Records 1. New York: Columbia University Press.

(1932) *The Vercelli Book*. Anglo-Saxon Poetic Records 2. New York: Columbia University Press.

Krapp, George Philip, and Elliott Van Kirk Dobbie, eds. (1936) *The Exeter Book*. Anglo-Saxon Poetic Records 3. New York: Columbia University Press.

MacLean, George Edwin, ed. (1884) Ælfric's Version of Alcuini interrogationes Sigeuulfi in Genesin. *Anglia* 7: 1–59.

Marsden, Richard, ed. (2008) *The Old English Heptateuch and Ælfric's Libellus de Veteri Testamento et Novo*, vol. 1: *Introduction and Text*. Early English Text Society original series 330. Oxford: Oxford University Press.

Maude, Kathryn, ed. and trans. (2017) *Berhtgyth's Letters to Balthard*. Medieval Feminist Forum Subsidia 7, Medieval Texts in Translation 4. https://scholarworks.wmich.edu/mff/vol53/iss3/1.

Meehan, Denis, ed. and trans. (1958, repr. 1983) *Adamnan's De locis sanctis*. Dublin: Dublin Institute for Advanced Studies.

Miller, Thomas, ed. (1890–8, repr. 1978) *The Old English Version of Bede's Ecclesiastical History of the English People*. Early English Text Society 95, 96, 110, 111. London; repr. Millwood, NY: Kraus Reprint.

O'Brien O'Keeffe, Katherine, ed. (2001) *The Anglo-Saxon Chronicle: A Collaborative Edition* vol. 5: *MS C*. Cambridge: Brewer.

Orchard, Andy. (1995) *Pride and Prodigies: Studies in the Monsters of the Beowulf-Manuscript*. Cambridge: Brewer.

Rauer, Christine, ed. and trans. (2013) *The Old English Martyrology: Edition, Translation and Commentary*. Anglo-Saxon Texts 10. Cambridge: Brewer.

Stevenson, William Henry, ed., reissued with article by Dorothy Whitelock. (1959) *Asser's Life of King Alfred Together with the Annals of Saint Neots*. Oxford: Clarendon.

Talbot, Charles Hugh, ed. and trans. (1954) *The Anglo-Saxon Missionaries in Germany: Being the Lives of SS. Willibrord, Boniface, Sturm, Leoba and Lebuin, together with the Hodoeporicon of St. Willibald and a Selection from the Correspondence of St. Boniface*. New York: Sheed and Ward.

Taylor, Simon, ed. (1983) *The Anglo-Saxon Chronicle: A Collaborative Edition* vol. 4: *MS B*. Cambridge: Brewer.

Wallis, Faith, ed. and trans. (1999) *Bede: The Reckoning of Time*. Translated Texts for Historians 29. Liverpool: Liverpool University Press.

Williamson, Craig. (1977) *The Old English Riddles of the Exeter Book*. Chapel Hill: University of North Carolina Press.

Secondary Texts

Abram, Christopher. (2010) New Light on the Illumination of Grendel's Mere. *Journal of English and Germanic Philology* 109(2): 198–216.

Anlezark, Daniel. (2002) Sceaf, Japheth and the Origins of the Anglo-Saxons. *Anglo-Saxon England* 31: 13–46.

  (2022) Alfred and the East. In Mark Atherton, Kazutomo Karasawa and Francis Leneghan, eds., *Ideas of the World in Early Medieval Literature.* Studies in Old English Literature 1. Turnhout: Brepols: 43–68.

Ben-Sasson, Haim Hillel, ed. (1976) *A History of the Jewish People.* Cambridge, MA: Harvard University Press.

Bosworth, Joseph. (1898, online 2014) *An Anglo-Saxon Dictionary Based on the Manuscript Collections of the Late Joseph Bosworth.* Ed. and enlarged by T. Northcote Toller. Oxford: Oxford University Press. Web version by Ondrej Tichy and Martin Rocek, Faculty of Arts, Charles University. https://bosworthtoller.com/.

Brady, Lindy. (2017) *Writing the Welsh Borderlands in Anglo-Saxon England.* Artes Liberales. Manchester: Manchester University Press.

Brooks, Kenneth R., ed. (1961) *Andreas and the Fates of the Apostles.* Oxford: Clarendon.

Bychowski, Gabrielle. (2018) Were There Transgender People in the Middle Ages? *The Public Medievalist.* www.publicmedievalist.com/transgender-middle-ages.

Cameron, Angus, Ashley Crandell Amos, Antonette diPaolo Healey et al. (2018) *The Dictionary of Old English: A to I Online.* Toronto: Dictionary of Old English Project.

Cohen, Jeffrey Jerome. (2003) *Medieval Identity Machines.* Minneapolis: University of Minnesota Press.

DeLoughrey, Elizabeth. (2014) Postcolonialism. In Greg Garrard, ed., *Oxford Handbook of Ecocriticism.* Oxford: Oxford University Press: 320–40.

Discenza, Nicole Guenther. (2002) The Old English *Bede* and the Construction of Anglo-Saxon Authority. *Anglo-Saxon England* 31: 69–80.

  (2017) *Inhabited Spaces: Anglo-Saxon Constructions of Place.* Toronto: University of Toronto Press.

Dockray-Miller, Mary. (2022). *Afrisc Meowle*: Exploring Race in the Old English *Exodus*. *PMLA* 137(3): 458–71.

Estes, Heide. (2007) Abraham and the Northmen in Genesis A: Alfredian Translations and Ninth-Century Politics. *Medievalia et Humanistica* 32: 1–13.

  (2017) *Anglo-Saxon Literary Landscapes: Ecotheory and the Environmental Imagination.* Amsterdam: Amsterdam University Press.

  (2021) Weather and the Creation of the Human in the Exeter Book Riddles. *Medieval Ecocriticisms* 1: 11–27. Special Issue, ed Michael J. Warren: "Medieval Weathers."

Fitzgerald, Jill. (Forthcoming) Afrisc meowle (*Exodus*). In Emily Butler and Irina Dumitrescu, eds., *Women in Early Medieval England: A Florilegium*. Palgrave.

Fleming, Robin. (2010) *Britain after Rome: The Fall and Rise, 400–1070*. New York: Penguin.

Foot, Sarah. (1996) The Making of *Angelcynn*: English Identity before the Norman Conquest. *Transactions of the Royal Historical Society*, 6th ser., 6: 25–49.

Foxhall Forbes, Helen. (2010) *Diuiduntur in quattuor*: The Interim and Judgement in Anglo-Saxon England. *The Journal of Theological Studies* NS 61, pt 2: 659–84.

(2013) *Heaven and Earth in Anglo-Saxon England: Theology and Society in an Age of Faith*. Farnham, Surrey: Ashgate.

Gardiner, Mark. (2011) Late Saxon Settlements. In Helena Hamerow, David A. Hinton, and Sally Crawford, eds., *The Oxford Handbook of Anglo-Saxon Archaeology*. Oxford: Oxford University Press: 198–217.

Giblett, Rod. (1996) *Postmodern Wetlands: Culture, History, Ecology*. Edinburgh: Edinburgh University Press.

Gneuss, Helmut, and Michael Lapidge. (2014) *Anglo-Saxon Manuscripts: A Bibliographical Handlist of Manuscripts and Manuscript Fragments Written or Owned in England up to 1100*. Toronto: University of Toronto Press.

Green, Caitlin R. (2015) The Medieval "New England": A Forgotten Anglo-Saxon Colony on the North-eastern Black Sea Coast. *Dr. Caitlin R. Green*. www.caitlingreen.org/2015/05/medieval-new-england-black-sea.html.

(2016a) Out of the Cold Far North and East? Some Oxygen Isotope Evidence for Scandinavian & Central/Eastern European Migrants in Britain, c. 2300 BC–AD 1050. *Dr. Caitlin R. Green*. www.caitlingreen.org/2016/01/oxygen-isotope-scandinavia.html.

(2016b) A Note on the Evidence for African Migrants in Britain from the Bronze Age to the Medieval Period. *Dr. Caitlin R. Green*. www.caitlingreen.org/2016/05/a-note-on-evidence-for-african-migrants.html.

Griffith, Mark, ed. (1997) *Judith*. Exeter: University of Exeter Press.

Hamerow, Helena. (2011) Anglo-Saxon Timber Buildings and Their Social Context. In Helena Hamerow, David A. Hinton, and Sally Crawford, eds., *The Oxford Handbook of Anglo-Saxon Archaeology*. Oxford: Oxford University Press: 156–71.

Harris, Stephen J. (2003) *Race and Ethnicity in Anglo-Saxon Literature*. Studies in Medieval History and Culture. New York: Routledge.

Healey, Antonette diPaolo, with John Price Wilkin and Xin Xiang. (2009) *The Dictionary of Old English Corpus on the World Wide Web*. Toronto: Dictionary of Old English Project.

Heng, Geraldine. (2018) *The Invention of Race in the European Middle Ages*. Cambridge: Cambridge University Press.

Hill, Thomas D. (1981) Invocation of the Trinity and the Tradition of the Lorica in Old English Poetry. *Speculum* 56(2): 259–67.

Howe, Nicholas. (1989) *Migration and Mythmaking in Anglo-Saxon England*. New Haven, CT: Yale University Press.

(2004) Rome: Capital of Anglo-Saxon England. *Journal of Medieval and Early Modern Studies* 34: 147–72.

(2008) *Writing the Map of Anglo-Saxon England: Essays in Cultural Geography*. New Haven, CT: Yale University Press.

Huggan, Graham, and Helen Tiffin. (2015) *Postcolonial Ecocriticism: Literature, Animals, Environment*. 2nd ed. New York: Routledge.

Hurley, Mary Kate. (2016) Distant Knowledge in the British Library, Cotton Tiberius B. v *Wonders of the East. Review of English Studies*, n.s. 67 (282): 827–43.

Kabir, Ananya Jahanara. (2001) *Paradise, Death and Doomsday in Anglo-Saxon Literature*. Cambridge Studies in Anglo-Saxon England 32. Cambridge: Cambridge University Press.

Karkov, Catherine E. (2020) *Imagining Anglo-Saxon England: Utopia, Heterotopia, Dystopia*. Cambridge: Cambridge University Press.

Kedwards, Dale. (2020) *The Mappae Mundi of Medieval Iceland. Studies in Old Norse Literature*. Cambridge: Brewer.

Keynes, Simon. (2014a) Appendix I: Rulers of the English, c.450–1066. In Michael Lapidge, John Blair, Simon Keynes, and Donald Scragg, eds., *The Wiley Blackwell Encyclopedia of Anglo-Saxon England*. 2nd ed. Malden, MA: Wiley Blackwell: 521–38.

(2014b) Cnut. In Michael Lapidge, John Blair, Simon Keynes, and Donald Scragg, eds., *The Wiley Blackwell Encyclopedia of Anglo-Saxon England*. 2nd ed. Malden, MA: Wiley Blackwell: 111–12.

Kim, Dorothy, and M. W. Bychowski. (2019) Visions of Medieval Trans Feminism: An Introduction. *Medievalist Feminist Forum* 55(1): 6–41.

Kim, Susan M. (2010) "If One Who Is Loved Is Not Present, A Letter May Be Embraced Instead": Death and the Letter of Alexander to Aristotle. *Journal of English and Germanic Philology* 109(1): 33–51.

Klein, Stacy S. (2006) *Ruling Women: Queenship and Gender in Anglo-Saxon Literature*. Notre Dame, IN: University of Notre Dame Press.

Lapidge, Michael. (2002) Byzantium, Rome and England in the Early Middle Ages. *Settimane di Studio* 49, *Roma fra Oriente e Occidente*: 363–400.

(2014) Hygeburg. In Michael Lapidge, John Blair, Simon Keynes, and Donald Scragg, eds., *The Wiley Blackwell Encyclopedia of Anglo-Saxon England*. 2nd ed. Malden, MA: Wiley Blackwell: 251.

Lapidge, Michael, et al., eds. (2014) *The Wiley Blackwell Encyclopedia of Anglo-Saxon England*. 2nd ed. Malden, MA: Wiley Blackwell.

Latham, R. E., D. R. Howlett, and R. K. Ashdowne, eds. (1975–2013) *The Dictionary of Medieval Latin from British Sources*. 17 vols. Oxford: Oxford University Press. https://logeion.uchicago.edu/lexidium.

Lewis, Charlton T., and Charles Short. (1879) *A Latin Dictionary*. Oxford: Clarendon. *Logeion*. https://logeion.uchicago.edu.

Lopez-Jantzen, Nicole. (2019) Between Empires: Race and Ethnicity in the Early Middle Ages. *Literature Compass* 16 (9/10): https://doi.org/10.1111/lic3.12542.

Mellinkoff, Ruth. (1981) *The Mark of Cain*. Berkeley: University of California Press.

Mittman, Asa Simon, and Susan M. Kim. (2013) *Inconceivable Beasts: The Wonders of the East in the Beowulf Manuscript*. Tempe: Arizona Center for Medieval and Renaissance Studies.

Monk, Christopher. (2013) A Context for the Sexualization of Monsters in the Wonders of the East. *Anglo-Saxon England* 41: 79–99.

Naismith, Rory. (2005) Islamic Coins from Early Medieval England. *Numismatic Chronicle* 165: 193–222.

O'Brien O'Keeffe, Katherine. (2001) Guthlac's Crossings. *Quaestio* 26: 1–26.

Ortenberg, Veronica. (1990) Archbishop Sigeric's Journey to Rome in 990. *Anglo-Saxon England* 19: 197–246.

The Oxford Dictionary of National Biography. (2021) Oxford: Oxford University Press.

Palmer, Clare. (2006) Stewardship: A Case Study in Environmental Ethics. In R. J. Berry, ed., *Environmental Stewardship: Critical Perspectives, Past and Present*. London: T&T Clark: 63–75.

Pelteret, David A. E. (2014) Eleventh-Century Anglo-Saxon Long-Haul Travelers: Jerusalem, Constantinople, and Beyond. In S. S. Klein, W. Schipper, and S. Lewis-Simpson, eds., *The Maritime World of the Anglo-Saxons*. Tempe, AZ: Arizona Center for Medieval and Renaissance Studies: 75–129.

Plumwood, Val. (1997) *Feminism and the Master of Nature*. New York: Routledge.

Rajabzadeh, Shokoofeh. (2019) The Depoliticized Saracen and Muslim Erasure. *Literature Compass* 16 (9/10): https://doi.org/10.1111/lic3.12548.

Rambaran-Olm, Mary. (2014) *John the Baptist's Prayer or The Descent into Hell from the Exeter Book: Text, Translation and Critical Study.* Cambridge: Brewer.

(2018) Anglo-Saxon Studies [Early English Studies], Academia and White Supremacy. *Medium.* https://medium.com/@mrambaranolm/anglo-saxon-studies-academia-and-white-supremacy-17c87b360bf3.

(2019) Misnaming the Medieval: Rejecting "Anglo-Saxon" Studies. *History Workshop.* www.historyworkshop.org.uk/misnaming-the-medieval-rejecting-anglo-saxon-studies.

(Summer/Autumn 2021) A Wrinkle in Medieval Time: Ironing Out the Problems of Periodization, Gatekeeping, and Exclusion in Early English Studies. *New Literary History* 52(3/4): 385–406.

Rowley, Sharon M. (2011) *The Old English Version of Bede's Historia ecclesiastica.* Anglo-Saxon Studies 16. Woodbridge: Boydell and Brewer.

Scarfe Beckett, Katherine. (2003) *Anglo-Saxon Perceptions of the Islamic World.* Cambridge Studies in Anglo-Saxon England 33. Cambridge: Cambridge University Press.

Scheil, Andrew P. (2004) *The Footsteps of Israel: Understanding Jews in Anglo-Saxon England.* Ann Arbor: University of Michigan Press.

(2016) *Babylon under Western Eyes: A Study of Allusion and Myth.* Toronto: University of Toronto Press.

Valtonen, Irmeli. (2008) *The North in the Old English Orosius: A Geographical Narrative in Context.* Helsinki: Modern Language Society of Helsinki.

Vernon, Matthew X. (2018) *The Black Middle Ages: Race and the Construction of the Middle Ages.* Cham: Palgrave Macmillan.

Wickham-Crowley, Kelley M. (2006) Living on the *Ecg*: The Mutable Boundaries of Land and Water in Anglo-Saxon Contexts. In Clare A. Lees and Gillian R. Overing, eds., *A Place to Believe in: Locating Medieval Landscapes.* University Park: Pennsylvania State University Press: 85–100.

Wilton, David. (2020) What Do We Mean by *Anglo-Saxon*? Pre-Conquest to the Present. *Journal of English and Germanic Philology* 119(4): 425–56.

Cambridge Elements ☰

England in the Early Medieval World

Megan Cavell
University of Birmingham

Megan Cavell is Associate Professor in medieval English literature at the University of Birmingham. She works on a wide range of topics in medieval literary studies, from Old and early Middle English and Latin languages and literature to riddling, gender and animal studies. Her previous publications include *Weaving Words and Binding Bodies: The Poetics of Human Experience in Old English Literature* (2016), *Riddles at Work in the Early Medieval Tradition: Words, Ideas, Interactions* (co-edited with Jennifer Neville, 2020), and *The Medieval Bestiary in England: Texts and Translations of the Old and Middle English Physiologus* (2022)

Rory Naismith
University of Cambridge

Rory Naismith is Professor of Early Medieval English History in the Department of Anglo-Saxon, Norse and Celtic at the University of Cambridge, and a Fellow of Corpus Christi College, Cambridge. Also a Fellow of the Royal Historical Society, he is the author of *Early Medieval Britain 500–1000* (Cambridge University Press, 2021), *Citadel of the Saxons: The Rise of Early London* (2018), *Medieval European Coinage, with a Catalogue of the Coins in the Fitzwilliam Museum, Cambridge, 8: Britain and Ireland c. 400–1066* (Cambridge University Press, 2017) and *Money and Power in Anglo-Saxon England: The Southern English Kingdoms 757–865* (Cambridge University Press, 2012, which won the 2013 International Society of Anglo-Saxonists First Book Prize).

Winfried Rudolf
University of Göttingen

Winfried Rudolf is Chair of Medieval English Language and Literature in the University of Göttingen (Germany). Recent publications include *Childhood and Adolescence in Anglo-Saxon Literary Culture* (with Susan E. Irvine, 2018). He has published widely on homiletic literature in early England and is currently principal investigator of the ERC-Project ECHOE–Electronic Corpus of Anonymous Homilies in Old English.

Emily V. Thornbury
Yale University

Emily V. Thornbury is Associate Professor of English at Yale University. She studies the literature and art of early England, with a particular emphasis on English and Latin poetry. Her publications include *Becoming a Poet in Anglo-Saxon England* (Cambridge, 2014), and, co-edited with Rebecca Stephenson, *Latinity and Identity in Anglo-Saxon Literature* (2016). She is currently working on a monograph called *The Virtue of Ornament*, about pre-Conquest theories of aesthetic value.

About the Series

Elements in England in the Early Medieval World takes an innovative, interdisciplinary view of the culture, history, literature, archaeology and legacy of England between the fifth and eleventh centuries. Individual contributions question and situate key themes, and thereby bring new perspectives to the heritage of early medieval England. They draw on texts in Latin and Old English as well as material culture to paint a vivid picture of the period. Relevant not only to students and scholars working in medieval studies, these volumes explore the rich intellectual, methodological and comparative value that the dynamic researchers interested in England between the fifth and eleventh centuries have to offer in a modern, global context. The series is driven by a commitment to inclusive and critical scholarship, and to the view that early medieval studies have a part to play in many fields of academic research, as well as constituting a vibrant and self-contained area of research in its own right.

Cambridge Elements ☰

England in the Early Medieval World